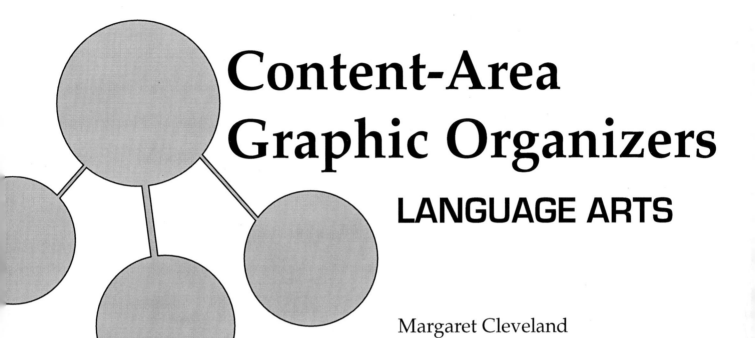

Content-Area
Graphic Organizers
LANGUAGE ARTS

Margaret Cleveland

WALCH PUBLISHING

1   2   3   4   5   6   7   8   9   10
ISBN 0-8251-4950-9
Copyright © 2005
J. Weston Walch, Publisher
P. O. Box 658 • Portland, Maine 04104-0658
walch.com
Printed in the United States of America

WALCH PUBLISHING

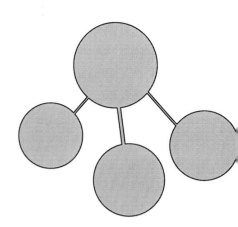

Table of Contents

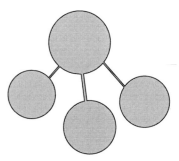

To the Teacher

Graphic organizers can be a versatile tool in your classroom. Organizers offer an easy, straightforward way to visually present a wide range of material. Research suggests that graphic organizers support learning in the classroom for all levels of learners. Gifted students, students on grade level, and students with learning difficulties all benefit from their use. Graphic organizers reduce the cognitive demand on students by helping them access information quickly and clearly. Using graphic organizers, learners can understand content more clearly and can take clear, concise notes. Ultimately, learners find it easier to retain and apply what they've learned.

Graphic organizers help foster higher-level thinking skills. They help students identify main ideas and details in their reading. They make it easier for students to see patterns such as cause and effect, comparing and contrasting, and chronological order. Organizers also help learners master critical-thinking skills by asking them to recall, evaluate, synthesize, analyze, and apply what they've learned. Research suggests that graphic organizers contribute to better test scores because they help students understand relationships between key ideas and enable them to be more focused as they study.

This book shows students how they can use some common graphic organizers as they read and write in language arts classes. As they become familiar with graphic organizers, they will be able to adapt them to suit their needs.

In the language arts classroom, graphic organizers help students:
- preview new material
- make connections between new material and prior learning
- recognize patterns and main ideas in reading
- understand the relationships between key ideas
- organize information and take notes
- review material
- prepare for the writing process

This book offers graphic organizers suitable for language arts tasks, grouped according to big-picture skills, such as organizing, categorizing, and classifying; comparing and contrasting; showing cause and effect; showing sequence and development; and writing. Each organizer is introduced with an explanation of its primary uses and structure. Next comes a step-by-step description of how to create the organizer, with a worked-out example that uses text relevant to the content area. Finally, an application section asks students to use the techniques they have just learned to complete a blank organizer with information from a sample text. Throughout, learners are encouraged to customize the organizers to suit their needs. To emphasize the variety of graphic organizers available, an additional organizer suitable for each big-picture skill is introduced briefly at the end of each lesson.

Content-Area Graphic Organizers for Language Arts is easy to use. Simply photocopy and distribute the section on each graphic organizer. Blank copies of the graphic organizers are included at the back of this book so that you can copy them as often as needed. The blank organizers are also available for download at our website, walch.com.

As learners become familiar with using graphic organizers, they will develop their own approaches and create their own organizers. Encourage them to adapt them, change them, and create their own for more complex strategies and connections. Remember, there is no one right way to use graphic organizers; the best way is the way that works for each student.

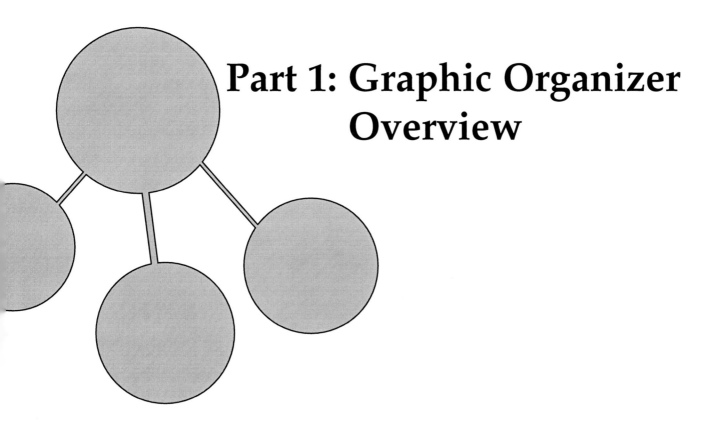

Part 1: Graphic Organizer Overview

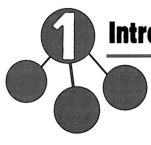

Introduction to Graphic Organizers

Welcome to the world of graphic organizers! If you've ever made a web or filled in a chart, then you already know how to use a graphic organizer. In this book, you'll explore a variety of graphic organizers and learn how to tailor them to meet your needs. And you'll find that they can make learning a lot easier!

You can use graphic organizers before you even begin a lesson. They can help you lay the foundation for new ideas. They also help you review what you've learned or already know about a subject, such as when you create a brainstorming web.

Graphic organizers are great tools when you are reading—they can help you through a poem, a story, a biography, or an informational article. Organizers help you analyze what you are reading. You can use them to recognize patterns in your reading, such as identifying the main idea of a story or an article, and finding the details that support the main idea. They can help you compare and contrast things within a story or between two stories. They can even be useful after you read. You can use them to organize your notes and figure out the most important points.

You can use graphic organizers when you write, too. They are particularly useful for prewriting and planning. Organizers can help you brainstorm new ideas and sort out the key points you want to make. Organizers are tools to focus your writing, and you can even use them to remember the steps of the writing process.

Graphic Organizers in English and Language Arts

In this book, you'll learn about graphic organizers that will help your reading and writing in language arts and English classes. Whether you are reading plays, poems, short stories, novels, or informational articles, you can use graphic organizers to get the most out of your work and time.

Graphic Organizers for Reading

Whenever you read a text or a story, you'll find that the author has organized the writing in a certain way. Normally in stories, the reading is organized in sequential order—there's a beginning, a middle, and an end. In informational writing, text may be organized in a number of ways. It may be written chronologically—in time order. It may be written to show a comparison between one event or character and another. The writing may be organized to show cause and effect—how one thing affects another. Recognizing these patterns of organization will help you understand your English and language arts reading.

Graphic organizers can help you recognize the patterns in your reading assignments. In this book, you'll use graphic organizers to
- organize, classify, and categorize information
- compare and contrast characters, events, or ideas
- understand cause and effect
- recognize and show story sequence and character development

Graphic Organizers for Writing

Graphic organizers don't just help you understand your reading. They can also be useful as you prepare to write an essay, a story, or a poem. They are particularly useful for planning in the prewriting stage. In this book, you'll learn how to brainstorm using a web. You'll also learn the best ways to outline, both formally and informally. Once you understand these prewriting skills, writing will be much easier.

As you learn how to use the organizers in this book, you can adapt them to suit your needs. Don't be afraid to get creative with them. Add rows and columns to tables, add circles to webs, or use different shapes. The only "correct" way to use graphic organizers is the way that suits your learning style. Graphic organizers are your tools, and you should make them work for you. Good luck!

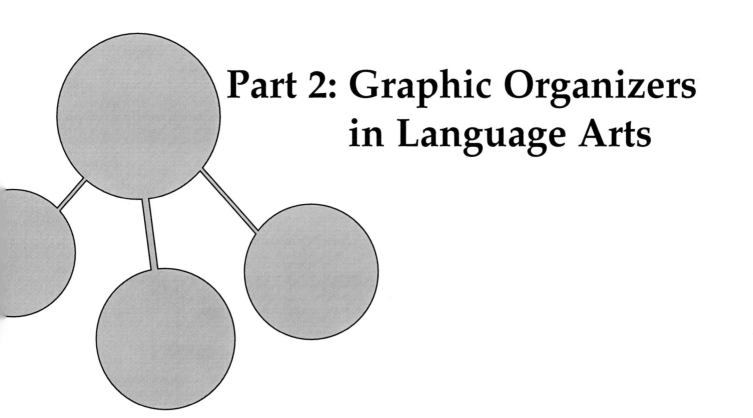

Part 2: Graphic Organizers in Language Arts

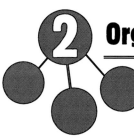

Organizing, Categorizing, and Classifying

Have you ever read an article and found the important points difficult to remember? Perhaps you've read a story and had a hard time keeping the characters or the plot straight. It can be frustrating to read a lot of information and get lost in the details! One of the best ways to sort out the important points in your reading is to use a graphic organizer. Two common organizers are webs and charts. With a web or chart, you can organize, classify, and categorize the key points you are reading. Webs and charts make it easy to remember what you've read and to decide what is the most important information in the reading.

Here's an example. Look at this list of animals: deer, dog, snake, cat, lizard, cow, iguana, alligator, and whale. Can you quickly remember all nine animals in the list? For most people, this would be a challenge. But what if you organized the list? First you would have to decide what makes sense—how to sort the animals. One way is to organize the animals into two categories: mammals and reptiles. A chart showing these two categories might look like this:

Mammals	Reptiles
deer	snake
dog	lizard
cat	iguana
cow	alligator
whale	

The information is categorized so that it is clear and easy to remember and understand. Now it is much easier to remember the list of animals.

Of course, this isn't the only way these animals can be grouped. The categories could be wild animals and domestic animals, or meat-eating and plant-eating animals. The important thing is to choose categories that make sense to you. That makes it easier for you to remember.

Another way you might remember the list of animals is to create a web. You can divide the list into two different areas—reptiles and mammals—under the main category "Animals." That way you can see how all the words are related to animals. Here's what a web of the list of animals might look like:

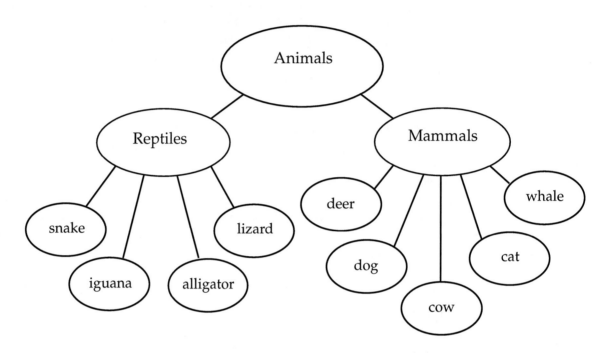

As you read, you can use graphic organizers to organize information much more complex than the list of animals above. You can use them to organize your thoughts before you read and to organize your notes while you are reading. You can also use them after you've read, to remember the main points.

In this lesson, we'll take an in-depth look at how to create the most common—and most useful—graphic organizers: webs and charts.

Webs   A web is a free-flowing graphic organizer that can be used to relate words, ideas, events, or characters.

Using Webs   Use webs before you read, while you are reading, and even after you read, to keep the information clear in your mind.

Before You Read   You can use webs before you read to identify what you already know about the subject. This process is important because it helps you think carefully about what you are going to read. Once you figure out what you already know, you can sort out what is new to you. For example, let's say you are about to read an article about the writer Mark Twain. Do you already know anything about him? Before you read the article, you can create a web by putting the main idea—Mark Twain—in the middle circle. Then you can add circles around the main idea to show what you already know.

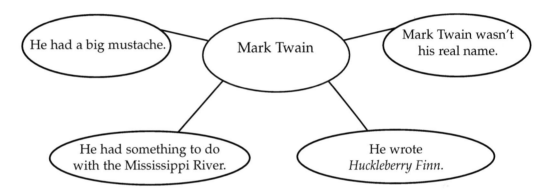

While You Read   While you read, you can add circles with facts or details as you learn them. Maybe you will add to the information you already know, or maybe you will create new circles around the main idea. Use what works best for you.

After You Read   After you read, you can look at your web and see clearly the main points in the article or story. The web will help you remember what you've read. It will also help you organize the information.

Webs in Action Below is an article about the life of Mark Twain. You'll see that the information from page 9 is filled in as facts already known about the writer. In some cases, the new information is added to the existing circles. In some cases, it is added as new circles. Take a look at the article and see how the important points are drawn around the main idea of "Mark Twain" in the web below.

A Brief History of Twain

"Mark twain! Mark twain!" The writer Samuel Clemens heard this call over and over again as he piloted a riverboat down the long, winding Mississippi River. The call means, "The water is two fathoms deep!" (A fathom is about six feet.) This call is used to help mariners navigate the uneven waters of the country's longest river. But Samuel Clemens had other plans for the call. He made it his *nom de plume*—his pen name—for the hundreds of articles and many novels he wrote in his lifetime.

Mark Twain was best known as a humorist and writer. His most famous work is *Huckleberry Finn*, read in classrooms and libraries all over the country. Twain was a unique character. He always dressed in white. In his later years, he sported a large white mustache. One of the most fascinating facts about Mark Twain is that in the year he was born, Halley's comet sped through the skies. Halley's comet can be seen only once every seventy-six years. Twain always said that he had "come in" with the comet and he planned to "go out" with the comet, too. Sure enough, he died the year the comet came back.

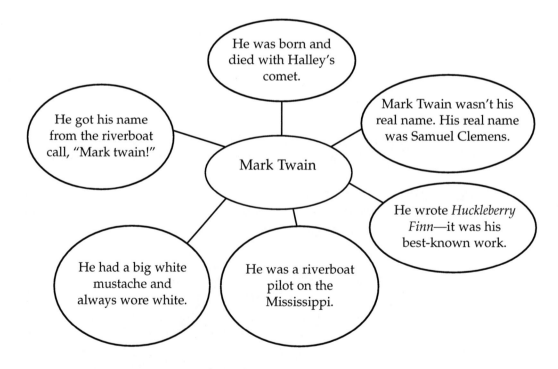

Application Below you'll find an article about the origin of newspapers. Do you know anything about early newspapers? If so, write what you know in the web on the next page. If not, don't worry; you'll learn some fascinating facts about newspapers as you go along. As you read, think carefully about what are the most important points of the article. Then transfer those points into brief phrases in the circles around the web to remind you of the important ideas you learned about newspapers.

Extra! Extra! Read All About It!

Before there were televisions, before the Internet, before radio, people looked to newspapers for their daily diet of news and information. But even newspapers haven't been around forever. And their history began many, many years ago.

The first newspapers were written more than 600 years ago—by hand! In Europe, merchants were the first people to write and read papers. They wrote about everything from war news to what people were buying and trading to social customs of the day. The first printed newspapers originated in Germany. These were accounts of dramatic or sensational events. One of the most famous accounts in a German newspaper was the story of the horrible Vlad Drakul, who tortured and mistreated Germans in neighboring Transylvania. Drakul, a real person, became the fictional character Count Dracula in novels and movies.

The first news reports printed in English were called *corantos.* These were brochures, or pamphlets, that were created when a big event happened. The *London Gazette* was the first official English-language newspaper, begun in England in 1666.

In the United States, the first newspaper was published in Boston in 1690, called *Publick Occurrences.* But the government did not like this paper. Printing was halted quickly. It wasn't until 1704 that the first truly successful paper, the *Boston News-Letter,* made its way into circulation in Boston. Shortly, papers sprang up in New York and in Philadelphia. By 1814 there were 346 newspapers in the United States.

Before the 1830s, printing newspapers was slow and expensive. The type for each letter was placed by hand. Printing presses were slow, and paper cost a great deal. Only the most educated and wealthy Americans could afford a subscription to a newspaper. After the 1830s, technology changed. It became easier, cheaper, and faster to print. Newspapers became inexpensive. They were available to anyone who could read. Those who couldn't read were inspired to learn so they could get the news of the day. In many ways, newspapers contributed to the fairly widespread literacy of nineteenth-century Americans.

Many historians argue that the newspaper is one of the true backbones of American history. The first article of the Bill of Rights, written in 1791, reads, "Congress shall make no law . . . abridging the freedom of speech or of the press." Newspapers are a key part of U.S. culture, history, politics, and society. The press—those who gather the news—is an important part of American society.

Web Use this web to organize the information from the reading on page 11.
Remember, the web should fit your needs; you can add or delete lines and
circles as you need to.

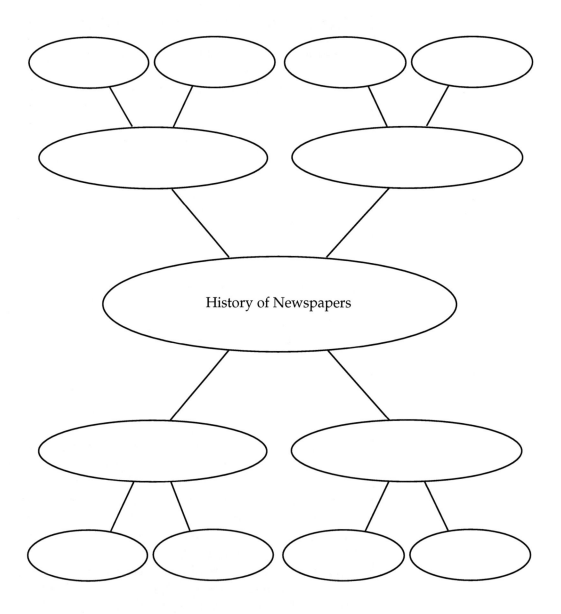

Charts   Another very useful graphic organizer is a chart. Compared with webs, charts are more structured ways to organize information. A chart begins with specific categories, and only the information that fits in those categories is included on the chart. Charts can also be called tables or matrix diagrams. Charts can be very simple, such as the T-chart. They can also be more complex, with five, six, or even more columns.

Using Charts   You can use a T-chart when you want to organize your thoughts into two main categories. For example, you can describe the pros and cons of a topic. You can evaluate the advantages and disadvantages of something. Or you can look at facts and opinions on any subject.

Here's an easy example. Let's say you and your family are thinking of taking a vacation. Some of the family thinks it would be fun to go camping. Some family members aren't sure about camping. You decide to create a T-chart to help you evaluate the pros and cons of a camping trip. The T-chart shows the pros on one side and the cons on the other.

Going on a Camping Vacation

Pros	Cons
fun family time	lots of work to carry tents and food
time spent outside	possible bad weather
get exercise	may be buggy
relaxing	could get boring
campfire at night	uncomfortable sleeping

A chart can help you condense complicated information into a simple form. It can help you see the differences and similarities between things. It can also help you identify facts or evaluate options. A chart can have any number of rows and columns, depending on what you are charting. For example, imagine that your teacher asks you to remember the definitions of several vocabulary words. He or she wants you to think about what each word means, based on the context. He or she has also asked you to look up each word. How will you keep all the information straight? A chart will help you sort it out and remember the meanings of the words.

To make a chart, the first step is to choose the words that go at the tops of the columns—the categories, or column heads. These words depend on the content you are charting. Ask yourself what you need to show in the chart. In this case, you need to list each vocabulary word, what you think it means, and the dictionary definition. You can use this to create your column heads. Then you would write each word in the first column—making the words your row heads—and what you think each word means in the second column. When you have done this for all the words, you could look them all up in the dictionary and fill in the last column.

Here is one student's example:

Vocabulary Word	What I Think It Means	Definition from Dictionary
consternation	stir up	a sudden, alarming amazement or dread that results in confusion; dread
levee	even or level	an embankment designed to prevent the flooding of a river
lavish	plentiful	occurring in abundance
uncanny	strange	mysterious; arousing fear or dread
virtually	completely	for the most part; wholly

Charts in Action Below is a short article discussing language techniques often found in fiction and poetry. While you're reading this article, it may be difficult to keep all the different techniques straight. It might also be hard to remember them. Constructing a chart is a great way to help you remember what the techniques are called and what they are used for.

As you read the article, think about what words you would choose for column and row heads. Then see a sample chart of the information.

Fictional Imagery

Writers use imagery—written words that create a mental picture—to help readers grasp the sights, smells, tastes, sounds, and textures in the story they are telling. Poets also use imagery to help readers feel the sensations they describe. This imagery is often created through the use of figurative language. Several techniques make up figurative language. Knowing them can help you analyze—and enjoy—what you read.

One of the most common techniques of figurative language is alliteration, in which the writer uses the same first consonant for many words in a line. Here's an example: *He clasps the crag with crooked claw.*

Simile is another common element of figurative language. Writers use similes to compare one thing to another, using the words "like" or "as." *She was as cold as an ice cube.* Metaphor is a cousin to simile—it is also a comparison, but it doesn't use "like" or "as": *He was a bear when it came to protecting his family.* Personification is a technique writers use when they give an inanimate object human qualities: *The wood stove sang when it was fed with wood.* Other common figurative language techniques include hyperbole, exaggerated statements—*He gave her a million presents for her birthday*—and onomatopoeia, a word that imitates the sound of the word, such as "buzz" or "hiss." As you read, look for some of these wonderful language elements. They truly will help you enjoy your reading!

This reader decided to use *Figurative Language Technique, Definition,* and *Example* for column heads, with the names of the techniques as row heads. Then, as she read about each technique, she filled in the information she needed.

Figurative Language Technique	Definition	Example
alliteration	words that repeat the same consonant at the beginning of each word	He clasps the crag with crooked claw.
simile	the comparison of two things, using "like" or "as"	She was as cold as an ice cube.
metaphor	the comparison of two things without using "like" or "as"	He was a bear when it came to protecting his family.
personification	a quality writers give inanimate objects to make them seem human	The wood stove sang when it was filled with wood.
hyperbole	exaggerated statements	He gave her a million presents for her birthday.
onomatopoeia	a word that imitates the sound of the word	hiss, buzz

Application Now it's your turn to create a chart to keep track of information you read. Below you'll read part of a description of two characters from American writer James Fenimore Cooper's *The Deerslayer*. The language is fairly complex, so you'll need to read carefully to determine the most important details about the two characters. Then fill in the chart on page 17. To get you started, we've listed categories for each row and filled in column heads including the "Evidence" column for you to note on what line you found the description. You just need to fill in the remaining spaces with information about the two characters, Hurry Harry and Deerslayer.

From *The Deerslayer* by James Fenimore Cooper

It would not have been easy to find a more noble specimen of vigorous manhood than was offered in the person of him who called himself Hurry Harry. His real name was Henry March . . . and not unfrequently he was termed Hurry Skurry, a nickname he had obtained from a dashing, reckless, off-hand manner, and a physical restlessness that kept him so constantly on the move. . . . The stature of Hurry Harry exceeded six feet four, and being unusually well proportioned, his strength fully realized the idea created by his gigantic frame. The face did no discredit to the rest of the man, for it was both good-humored and handsome. His air was free, and though his manner necessarily partook of the rudeness of a border life, the grandeur that pervaded so noble a physique prevented it from becoming altogether vulgar.

Deerslayer, as Hurry called his companion, was a very different person in appearance, as well as in character. In stature he stood about six feet in his moccasins, but his frame was comparatively light and slender, showing muscles, however, that promised unusual agility, if not unusual strength. His face would have had little to recommend it except youth. . . . This expression was simply that of guileless truth, sustained by an earnestness of purpose, and a sincerity of feeling, that rendered it remarkable. . . .

Both these frontiersmen were still young, Hurry having reached the age of six or eight and twenty, while Deerslayer was several years his junior. Their attire needs no particular description, though it may be well to add that it was composed in no small degree of dressed deer-skins. . . . There was, notwithstanding, some attention to smartness and the picturesque in the arrangements of Deerslayer's dress, more particularly in the part connected with his arms and accoutrements. His rifle was in perfect condition, the handle of his hunting-knife was neatly carved, his powder-horn was ornamented with suitable devices lightly cut into the material, and his shot-pouch was decorated with wampum. On the other hand, Hurry Harry . . . wore everything in a careless, slovenly manner, as if he felt a noble scorn for the trifling accessories of dress and ornaments.

Chart Use this chart to organize the information from the reading on page 16. Remember, the chart should fit your needs; you can change or add column and row heads if you need to.

	Hurry Harry	Deerslayer	Evidence
Physical description			
How he dresses			
Other characteristics			
What his personality might be like based on his description			

Main Idea and Details Chart

Have you ever read an article and then, when you were finished reading, wondered what it was really about? Or have you ever read something, only to forget it soon after? If you answered yes to either question, you are not alone. Luckily, there is a skill you can use to help you understand and enjoy what you read.

Finding the main idea and supporting details is perhaps the most important reading skill. Without this skill, you will not be able to remember or even understand what you read. Luckily, it is not too difficult to locate the main idea and details. And charting them in a main idea and details chart is a quick way to bring all of the key ideas together.

Using Main Idea and Details Charts

The best way to locate the main idea is to identify the topic sentence in each paragraph of your reading. Be sure that you understand what the topic sentence means. Next, you need to find the details that support the main ideas. What facts or evidence can you find that makes the main idea credible?

17

Here's an example. Read the following paragraph and determine the main idea and the supporting details. Then look at the completed main idea and details chart that follows.

The Art of Fencing

Fencing is a sport—and an art—enjoyed by all age groups in the United States. Fencers use dulled swords to compete with one another in team and individual events. Fencers use three different types of weapons. The foil is a slender, flexible sword used in competition. Those who use a foil in fencing score by touching their opponent in the torso with the blunted point. Épée fencing uses a more rigid blade, and scoring is counted when a player touches the opponent anywhere on the body. The saber is a shorter blade than the other swords, and points are scored when a player touches an opponent above the hips, including the head and arms. Fencing is an established Olympic sport.

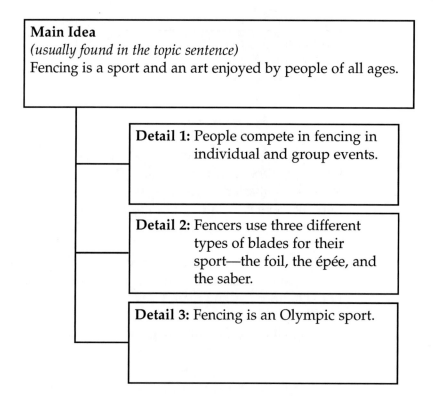

Main Idea
(usually found in the topic sentence)
Fencing is a sport and an art enjoyed by people of all ages.

Detail 1: People compete in fencing in individual and group events.

Detail 2: Fencers use three different types of blades for their sport—the foil, the épée, and the saber.

Detail 3: Fencing is an Olympic sport.

Main Idea and Details Charts in Action Your assignments won't always be as simple as one paragraph with an obvious topic sentence and only a few follow-up sentences as details. But generally the pattern will be the same. Read the text below and see how the main idea and details have been charted.

Never Too Young to Publish

Have you ever wanted to publish a poem, a photo, a piece of creative writing, or even an essay? Many young writers believe they must have years of experience before they can publish their work. But plenty of magazines, web sites, and other periodicals are eager for teens to submit their work for publication.

One of the best resources for information on getting published is *The Young Writer's Guide to Getting Published* by Kathy Henderson. This book, published by Writer's Digest Books, outlines the many marketplaces where young writers can submit their work, including magazines and web sites.

But you may want to submit your work directly to one of the magazines best known for publishing teen work. One magazine, *Cicada*, focuses on first-person essays, short stories, and poems created by writers fourteen and older. *TeenInk* is a monthly magazine for teens to submit photos, art, poems, stories, or nonfiction reviews. *Spire Magazine* highlights work by writers under twenty-one who come from disadvantaged or minority backgrounds. Their motto is that they are supporting artists who will "create the future of arts and literature."

These days there are also several web sites devoted to submissions by young authors. Writing.com, for example, was established in 2000. Since then, it has attracted a following of thousands of writers. With more than 16,000 pages in submissions, Writing.com is one of the largest on-line publishers of new material.

So if you are considering publishing that poem or story, do it! Check out one of the avenues for publishing, and experience the thrill of seeing your name in print!

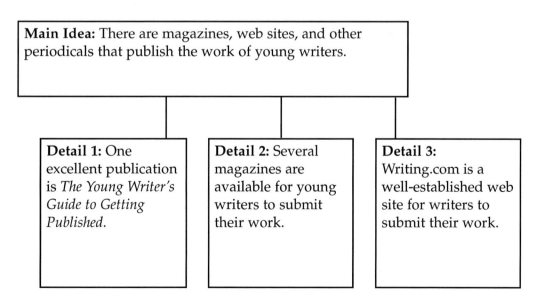

Main Idea: There are magazines, web sites, and other periodicals that publish the work of young writers.

Detail 1: One excellent publication is *The Young Writer's Guide to Getting Published.*

Detail 2: Several magazines are available for young writers to submit their work.

Detail 3: Writing.com is a well-established web site for writers to submit their work.

Application Now chart the main idea and details of the article below about the famous pilot, horse trainer, and writer, Beryl Markham. In this case, you may want to chart more than one main idea. The blank chart on page 21 offers enough space for three main ideas and several supporting details for each main idea.

Braving the Odds

Ernest Hemingway wrote, "She can write rings around any of us who consider ourselves writers." He wrote this about Beryl Markham, the maverick aviator whose book *West with the Night* topped the best-seller charts upon its publication in 1942.

But writing wasn't the only thing Beryl Markham did well. As a child, growing up in Kenya, she was taught how to handle horses on her father's farm, and she grew up to become an accomplished horse trainer. At just twenty-four, she won a coveted horse-training prize and was launched into the elite British society that ruled Kenya at the time. She met and married Mansfield Markham, a wealthy Englishman. The marriage ended after a short time, and Beryl Markham continued her career.

Then she met Dennis Finch Hatton, an English game hunter, who shared his passion for flying with her. Markham caught his enthusiasm and soon earned her pilot's license. Her new career was launched.

Markham became a bush pilot in Kenya, one who escorts hunters, supplies, and mail to remote areas. She flew without fear, on her own, landing often in open fields or small clearings.

But Beryl was still to make her mark in aviation history. In 1936, when she was thirty-four, she decided to try a feat no one—man or woman— had attempted before. She decided to fly from London to New York, across the Atlantic, against the strong headwinds that would make the trip slower and more dangerous than a west-to-east crossing. On September 4, she took off from London and traveled safely until one of her fuel lines froze and she began a plunge toward the freezing Atlantic waters. Just as she was about to crash, the line defrosted, and she once again soared toward New York. But again, a fuel line froze, and the second time, she was not so lucky. She crash landed on Nova Scotia, just off the coast of the United States.

The story is that she crashed into a muddy bog, stepped out gingerly, and announced to two very surprised fisherman, "I'm Mrs. Markham. I've just flown from England." And even though she didn't make it all the way, she attracted worldwide attention and was hailed as a hero.

Markham talked of entering other races, but when a dear friend was killed in an air crash, she stopped flying. She lived for a short time in California, where she started an avocado farm, but then returned to Kenya. She also returned to her first love, training horses.

Markham wrote of her flying adventures in Africa in her book *West with the Night*. Critics believe the book was cowritten by her third husband, Raoul Schumacher. But no one could coauthor the adventurous spirit of independence and triumph that made Beryl Markham a true heroine for generations to come.

Main Idea and Details Chart

Use this chart to organize the information from the reading on page 20. Write one main idea in each large box. Write supporting details in the smaller boxes. Remember, the chart should fit your needs; you can add or delete lines and boxes if you need to.

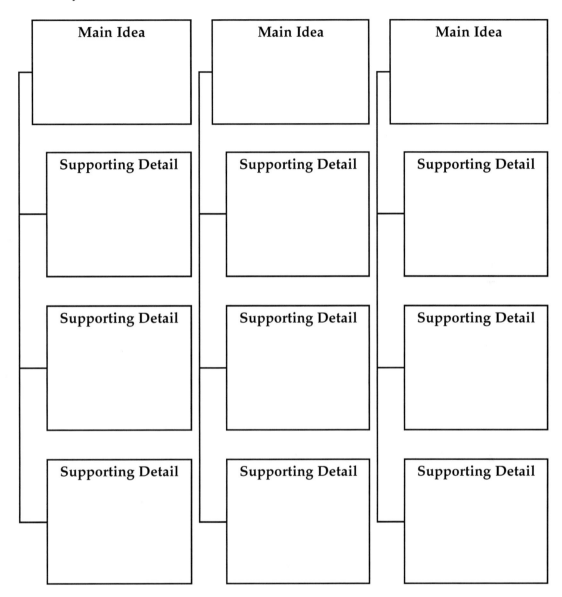

Spider Maps We have looked at three types of organizers in this section, but there are lots of other ways to organize information for reading assignments. Here is another organizer you could use to show the main idea and details of a story. Experiment with different ways to set up graphic organizers to find what works best for you.

Write the topic or theme of the reading in the oval. Write one main idea on each diagonal line. Add or delete lines as needed.

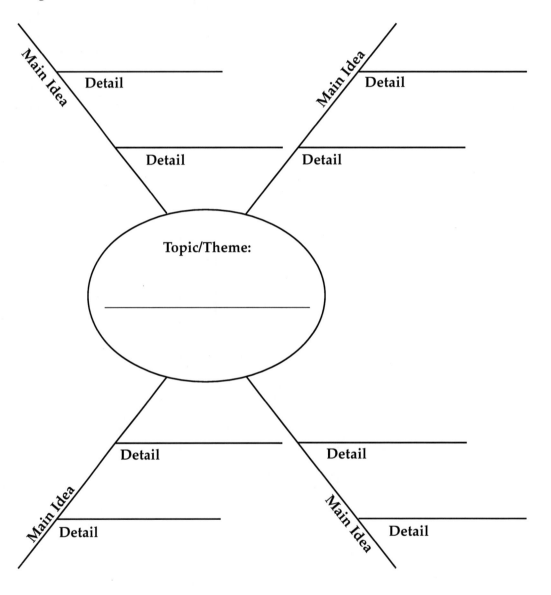

3 Comparing and Contrasting

Has your teacher ever asked you to compare and contrast characters in a story? Perhaps you have been asked to compare two stories by the same author, or maybe to contrast different authors and their styles. To compare means to find ways that things are alike. To contrast means to find ways that things are different. In language arts classes, you are often asked to compare and contrast characters, ideas, themes, essays, and plots. Comparing and contrasting is a skill that helps you organize and arrange information, making it easier to understand. Teachers often ask questions about comparing and contrasting on tests. It's a good idea to be prepared by using this skill in your reading!

One of the best ways to show how ideas, characters, plot events, or themes are different or alike is to chart them in a graphic organizer. Several different types of graphic organizers are useful for comparing and contrasting. One very simple organizer is called the Venn diagram. Another is the comparison matrix. In this lesson, you will learn how to use these compare and contrast organizers to help you improve your reading skills.

Venn Diagrams The Venn diagram has been around for more than 150 years. It is named after John Venn, who lived in the mid-1800s. Venn was a historian and an inventor. He developed the Venn diagram as a way to illustrate math and logic problems. Today, people use Venn diagrams to compare and contrast many different ideas. Venn diagrams are particularly useful in language arts to compare characters, stories, poems, themes, settings, and plots. They also can be used to compare whole books or differing points of view in informational reading.

Using Venn Diagrams

The Venn diagram is made by drawing two or more intersecting circles. The parts of the circles that overlap represent the ways that the things you are comparing are alike. The parts of the circles that do not overlap represent the way things are different.

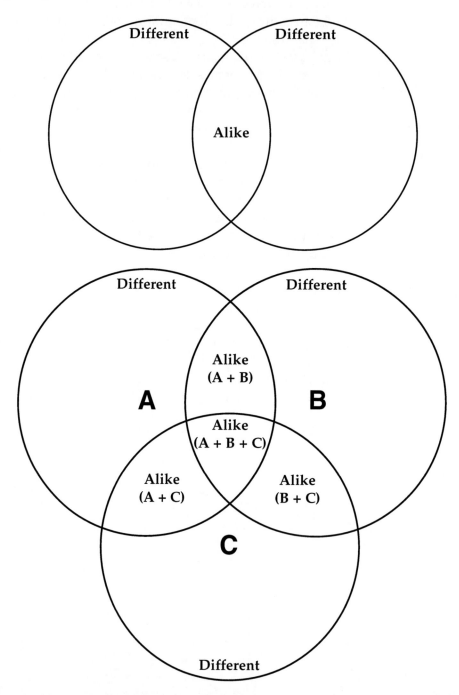

The most important thing to do when you need to compare and contrast is to ask yourself, "What is being compared?" Then ask yourself these questions: In what ways are the two things alike? In what ways are they different? Once you answer those questions, you can put the answers in the correct segments of the Venn circles.

Venn Diagrams in Action

Imagine that your teacher has asked you the question, "In what ways are poems like stories? In what ways are they different?"

Remember, the first thing you have to do is be sure you understand what you are being asked to compare. In this example, the question is clear. You are being asked to compare poems and stories. Begin by drawing your diagram. Put "poems" in the open area of one circle and "stories" in the other. Next, fill in the ways that poems and stories are different. Finally, go to the middle segment and fill in the ways that poems and stories are alike. See if you can add anything to the example below.

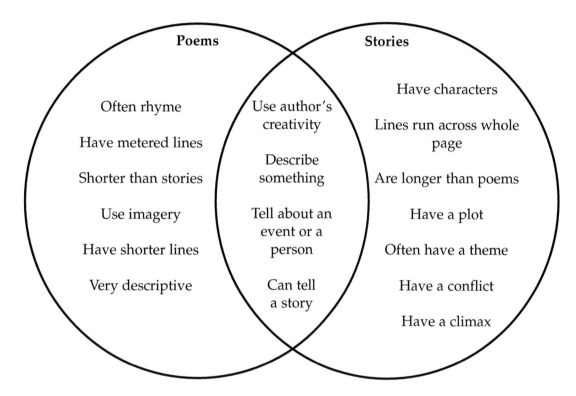

Application Now it's your turn to create and fill in a Venn diagram. Read the article below about the differences and similarities between colleges and universities. Remember to ask yourself these questions: What is being compared? What are the similarities? What are the differences? Then complete the Venn diagram on the next page.

College or University?

Introductory Question?

Are you planning to go to college? This is a question you'll often hear as you near the middle of your high-school education or as you complete your GED. But what if you want to go somewhere that is called a university? Would that be better than going to college? What's the difference? What are the similarities? Does one offer a better education?

1

Colleges and universities have many things in common. They are both places you go after graduating from high school or after you have scored well on the GED. Colleges and universities both offer a bachelor's degree once you've taken and passed all your courses. You can earn a bachelor of arts degree if most of your classes are history, philosophy, English, or fine arts. Or you can earn a bachelor of science. This is the degree you get when you study math, any of the sciences, or music.

2

Admission to colleges and universities is basically the same. Highly ranked colleges or universities tend to be harder to get into. But a college isn't necessarily harder to get into than a university—or vice versa.

3

Colleges and universities can be private or public. If they are public, they receive funding from their state government. If they are private, they rely on admission fees and money donated from people who have already graduated.

1

But colleges and universities are different, too. Colleges tend to be smaller, and classes are usually taught only by college teachers. Universities generally tend to be larger than colleges. Sometimes university classes are taught by graduate students. There are no graduate students at colleges. Only universities offer degrees higher than bachelor's degrees, such as a master's degree or a doctor of philosophy, known as a Ph.D.

2

Universities often split their faculty attention between teaching and research. Sometimes colleges are contained within a university, such as Harvard College, which is a division of Harvard University.

Conclusion

So which will you choose? Is a small college your choice? Or do you prefer a larger university where you can earn advanced degrees? Whatever you choose, it won't matter if it's a university or a college. Either way, you're bound to get a good education if you dedicate yourself to your studies.

Venn Diagram   Use this diagram to compare and contrast the information in the reading on page 26. Label each circle. Write things that are unique to each topic in the open area of each circle. Write things both topics have in common in the intersecting area.

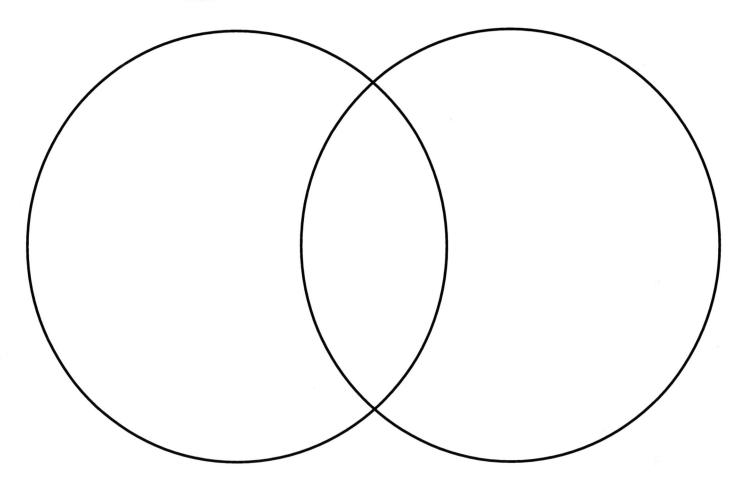

Comparison Matrixes

Another useful graphic organizer for comparing and contrasting is a comparison matrix. Use a comparison matrix when you want to link traits or characteristics. These characteristics might belong to a person, a place, a thing, an idea, or an event. A comparison matrix looks like a chart because it has rows and columns. However, the use of a comparison matrix is more limited than a chart. In a comparison matrix, one set of heads always lists the items to be compared. The other set always shows the characteristics you are comparing.

Using Comparison Matrixes

A comparison matrix is a little more complex than a Venn diagram. To use a comparison matrix, you have to think critically about what you want to compare. You should always ask yourself three important questions before you fill in your matrix:

1. What specific people/events/ideas/things am I comparing?

2. What specific characteristics am I comparing?

3. In what way are the items I am comparing alike and different, based on their characteristics?

Here is an example of a comparison matrix. In this case, we used the items being compared for row heads and the characteristics as column heads.

	Religion	Length of Holiday	In Celebration of	Gift-Giving Tradition
Christmas				
Hanukkah				
Kwanza				

Depending on the items you are comparing, you might put the items across the top and the characteristics along the side. If you had three items and nine characteristics, using the items as the row heads would make the most sense. Choose the orientation that fits your material best.

Comparison Matrixes in Action

Here's an everyday use for a comparison matrix. Imagine that you want to compare the hobbies of a family. The people being compared are different family members. Their names are placed at the start of each row. The characteristics being compared are the hobbies. They are placed at the top of each column. Here's how that might look in a comparison matrix.

	Reading	Sports	Cooking	Musical Instrument
Grandma	X		X	X
Dad	X	X	X	X
Tamara (older sister)		X		X
Luis (older brother)	X			X
Rhea (younger sister)				X

What does this comparison matrix tell you about this family? When you scan the matrix, you can see that everyone in the family enjoys playing a musical instrument. The matrix has made it easy to see how the hobbies of people in the household are alike and how they are different.

Application Now it is your turn to create and fill out a comparison matrix. Read the text below that describes the two characters from Ray Bradbury's novel *Something Wicked This Way Comes.* Even if you haven't read the novel, you will be able to tell enough about the characters to create a matrix.

Remember to ask yourself these three questions:

1. What specific people/events/ideas/things am I comparing?

2. What specific characteristics am I comparing?

3. In what way are the items I am comparing alike and different, based on their characteristics?

Then use the information to fill in the comparison matrix on page 31.

This Side of Midnight

Will Holloway and Jim Nightshade love each other. After all, they are best friends. Yet the two boys couldn't be more different. The differences in their characters make Ray Bradbury's *Something Wicked This Way Comes* a powerful science-fiction story.

Will and Jim begin their lives together by being born just minutes apart. Will is born moments before midnight on October 30. Jim is born moments after midnight—on October 31. The chilly, often haunting darkness of fall is the setting for the book.

The two boys are very different in appearance. Will is blond, pale, and slight. Jim is dark and strong.

The boys are also different in the way they act. Will is thoughtful and deliberate. He makes decisions slowly and carefully. He seems to enjoy thinking more than doing. Jim, on the other hand, is a quick thinker. He also acts quickly, often on impulse.

Will is a very empathetic person. He appears to feel the pain of other people. When one of the most wicked characters in the book dies, Will still feels sadness and remorse. Jim, on the other hand, does not have the same level of empathy for others. It is not that he is a bad person, but he doesn't have the same sensitivity as his friend Will. Jim believes that if he can't get hurt by something, then it isn't bad. Will understands that sometimes wickedness can be hidden below the surface.

The story of *Something Wicked This Way Comes* is about the way that Will and Jim deal with the temptation of evil. The boys are mirrors of the way most people think and act. On one hand, people can be careful and deliberate, like Will. On the other hand, they can be impulsive, like Jim. Together the boys are a representation of the way people struggle with good and evil throughout their lives.

Comparison Matrix   Use this comparison matrix to compare the characters in the reading on page 30. Remember, the chart should fit your needs; you can add or delete rows and columns if you need to.

Compare and Contrast Diagrams

We have looked at two compare and contrast organizers in this section, but there are lots of other ways to compare and contrast information. Here is another organizer you could use. Experiment with different ways to set up graphic organizers to find the ones that work best for you.

Write the things you are comparing on the lines at the top. In the first box, say how they are alike. Write the characteristics you are contrasting under "With Regard To." Then show how the items are different according to these characteristics.

Item 1 _____   Item 2 _____

How Alike?

_____
_____
_____
_____
_____

How Different?

With Regard To

_____   ⟷   _____
_____   ⟷   _____
_____   ⟷   _____
_____   ⟷   _____
_____   ⟷   _____

Showing Cause and Effect

If your alarm clock doesn't go off in the morning, you will probably be late for school or work. If you go outside in the winter without a coat, you will be cold. If you sow a seed in the early spring, a plant will grow. All of these statements represent an important relationship—cause and effect.

In the cause and effect relationship, the cause always comes first. The effect is always a result of the cause. These are the causes for the statements above:

- Your alarm clock doesn't go off.
- You go outside in winter without a coat.
- You sow a seed.

These are the effects:

- You are late for school or work.
- You are cold.
- A plant grows.

Recognizing cause and effect helps us understand why things happen in our reading and in our everyday lives. In your reading, you can look for key words that signal cause and effect. These are some common key words and phrases:

accordingly	due to	so that
as a result	for this reason	then
because	if…then	therefore
consequently	since	thus

When these signal words are not in the text, you will have to infer the cause of the events. When you infer, you make your best guess based on your knowledge and experience. The best way to make an inference is to ask yourself two important questions:

1. What happened? (This is the effect.)

2. Why did it happen? (This is the cause.)

You can use a graphic organizer to understand the cause and effect relationship between two events. In this lesson, you will learn about two common and useful graphic organizers: the cause and effect map and the fishbone diagram.

Cause and Effect Maps

A cause and effect map illustrates the relationship between the effect and the cause. It can be used to organize the plot of a story. You can also use it to help sort out the events of an informational story.

The format of cause and effect maps is flexible. For example, you can create a chart that lists just one effect. Then you can compose the list of causes that led to the event. You can also make a chart that shows one cause and several effects.

For example, suppose you lived in a place where there was a huge snowfall. What are some of the events that would happen as a result of the snowfall? If you were to create a simple cause and effect map, it might look like this:

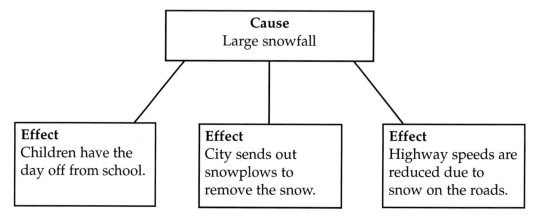

Sometimes there is more than one cause and more than one effect. In this case, you might use a cause-and-effect map like this:

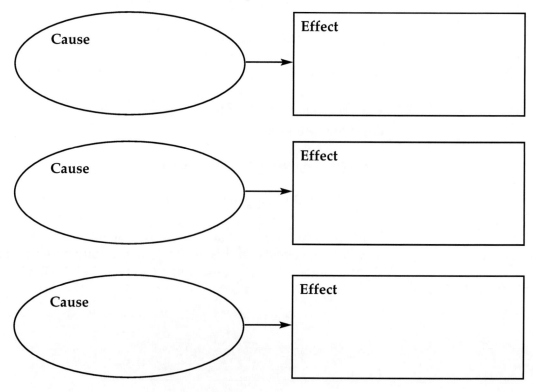

Cause and Effect Maps in Action

Here is an example of how you might use a cause and effect map. Read the sample below. Underline any cause-and-effect signal words. Then see how the cause and effect graphic organizer is filled out.

Girls of Invention

You don't have to be an adult to come up with bright ideas for new products. In fact, some very interesting things were invented by children—some under the age of ten!

When Chelsea Lannon was in kindergarten, she watched her mother change her brother's diaper over and over again. Her mother wrestled with the wipe and the powder and the diaper, often all with one hand! Chelsea came up with a new type of diaper—one with a little pocket. That way, everything her mother needed would be in one handy place. Chelsea was just eight when she received a patent for her invention.

Suzanna Goodin's daily chore was feeding her cat. Part of that job meant cleaning off the cat food spoon—a messy, smelly job. Suzanna came up with a great idea. She decided to create a spoon that her cat could eat. So she invented an edible spoon, made out of a dried cat food cracker—no more messy spoons!

And Becky Schroeder was only fourteen when she invented a way to use glow-in-the-dark paint underneath her writing paper so she could write at night. Today, astronauts use this process to read their manuals when there is no power. Doctors use it, too, to read medical charts at night without waking the patients.

Perhaps you have an invention waiting to happen. What will you invent?

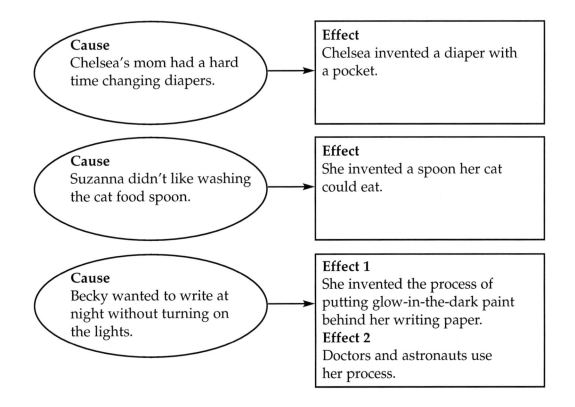

Application Now it's your turn to create a cause and effect graphic organizer. Read the following article about the writer Roald Dahl. Remember to look for signal words to help you find the causes and effects. Also ask yourself the questions: What happened? What caused it to happen? Then fill out the graphic organizer on the next page.

Life Imitating Art

If you've ever read *Charlie and the Chocolate Factory* or *James and the Giant Peach* (or seen their film adaptations), then you are familiar with the work of Roald Dahl. Dahl began his career as a serious writer of stories for adults, but he is best known for his quirky children's stories. Much of Dahl's own life is reflected in his stories.

Dahl didn't intend to be a writer. He was a pilot during World War II and expected to go into business after the war. But one day a writer asked Dahl to have lunch with him and to tell him about some of his flying adventures. The writer was eating and asked Dahl to jot down some notes for him. Then Dahl agreed to finish up the notes after the lunch. He finished up the notes and then created a story for his friend. He had enjoyed the task so much and was so good at it that he decided to keep writing. His first story, called "A Piece of Cake," was a result of that lunch. From there he went on to write many short stories for adults and for children.

When Dahl was a child, his sister died tragically. His father never recovered from his grief. He became distant, and Dahl felt that his father was not really there for him. As a result of his own experience, several of Dahl's characters are orphaned or are neglected by their parents.

Dahl also was a rebellious child. He questioned his teachers and the strict principals at his schools. He felt that those in charge at his schools were more interested in controlling the students than in teaching them. Because of his own experiences, Dahl brings this theme to several of his stories, such as *Matilda.*

One of Dahl's greatest loves was chocolate. When he was young, the Cadbury chocolate company came to his school to test their new products. Dahl and his classmates looked forward to these "tests." No doubt it was from these visits that the idea for *Charlie and the Chocolate Factory* was born.

Most writers call on their own experiences to form their stories. Dahl's slightly odd childhood is clearly represented in his eccentric stories that continue to charm readers of all ages.

Cause and Effect Map

Use this graphic organizer to show the causes and effects in the reading on page 36. Write each cause in one oval. Write all its effects in the box. Add or delete ovals and boxes as needed.

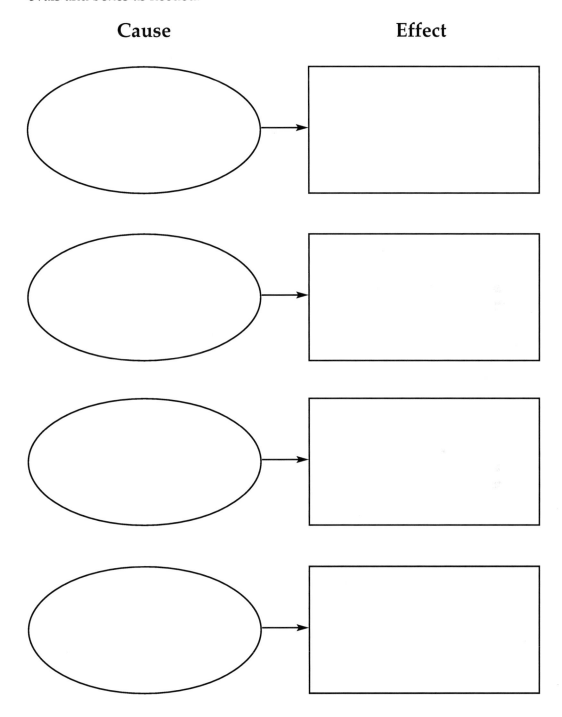

Cause   **Effect**

Fishbone Maps

Another useful graphic organizer is the fishbone map. The fishbone map is a bit more complex than the cause and effect map. The fishbone map illustrates several causes that produce a certain result.

Using Fishbone Maps

The fishbone map begins with a result. This is similar to the effect in the cause and effect map. Then come the causes that led to the event.

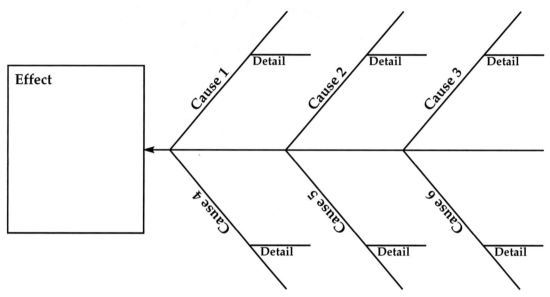

Fishbone Maps in Action

Here's an example of a fishbone map. You go to the grocery store and find that the price of oranges and orange juice is sky high. This is the effect. The first question you need to ask is, "Why did this event take place?" Think of some causes for the high prices. One possible reason is that the cost of transporting oranges to your supermarket is high. Then ask why again: Why might transportation costs be high? The answer could be that the price of gas has gone up, so it's more expensive to transport oranges. What might be another reason prices are higher? Farm workers asked for more pay, so orchard owners needed to charge more to cover the cost of paying the workers. Another reason could be that the crop didn't do as well as was expected. In this case, farmers might have to charge more to cover other expenses, like farming equipment, labor, and maintenance. These are just some of the reasons you might think of.

Here's how the reasons listed on the previous page can be shown in a fishbone map:

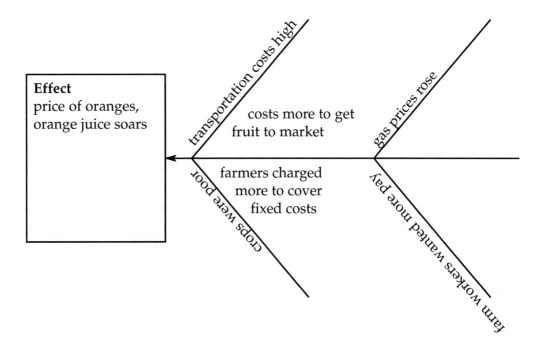

Application Do you know the story of the sinking of *Titanic*? Read the informational article below. Then fill in the fishbone map on page 41. Remember to ask yourself: What is the result? What made the result happen? Also remember to support your causes with as many details as you can.

The Day *Titanic* Went Down

April 15, 1912, was a very sad day. This was the day that the mammoth ocean liner *Titanic* hit an iceberg and sank, and 1,503 people were lost at sea.

Titanic was the largest ship ever built. Those who built it said it was "practically unsinkable." This was a popular notion spread by the media. People believed it to be true. The irony was that the ship did sink due to several mistakes made by the builders, the captain, and the crew.

Calm seas are usually considered a good thing at sea. But calm seas in cold air make icebergs almost invisible from a distance. It is only when the seas are churning that foam around the giant ice islands makes them visible from far away. The crew, who were on lookout without proper binoculars, did not see the iceberg that gouged *Titanic* until it was too late to turn the ship away. And while the ship was not going at full speed, it was still traveling faster than recommended, making it impossible to turn at short notice.

Other crew errors added to the fate of the ship. Radio operators did not follow up with officers about reports describing icebergs in their path. Many of the staff who worked on the ship had been hired just before *Titanic* set sail, so they were not trained properly. And when the ship struck the iceberg, crew members tried to keep passengers calm and downplayed the danger. As a result, many of the lifeboats left without being filled.

Design and planning issues also contributed to *Titanic*'s sad end. There were only enough lifeboats aboard for a ship that weighed a quarter of what *Titanic* weighed. Still, shipping regulations stated that the ship needed just sixteen lifeboats. The White Star Line, *Titanic*'s managing company, had added four more, just to be on the safe side.

Titanic had other design flaws as well. The structure of the ship between the third and fourth funnels was the weakest on the ship. This spot is precisely where the iceberg struck. The bolts used to fasten the steel hulls were of poor quality and were unstable at freezing temperatures.

While the sinking of *Titanic* is tragic, some lessons were learned from this disaster. Lifeboat standards changed to ensure the safety of all passengers. Radio contact with the shore and other ships is required throughout a ship's voyage. Now caution is always the rule rather than the exception.

Fishbone Map   Use this fishbone map to show the causes and effects in the reading on page 40.

Write the effect in the box at the left. Write the causes on the diagonal lines.
Write details on the short horizontal lines. Add or delete lines as needed.

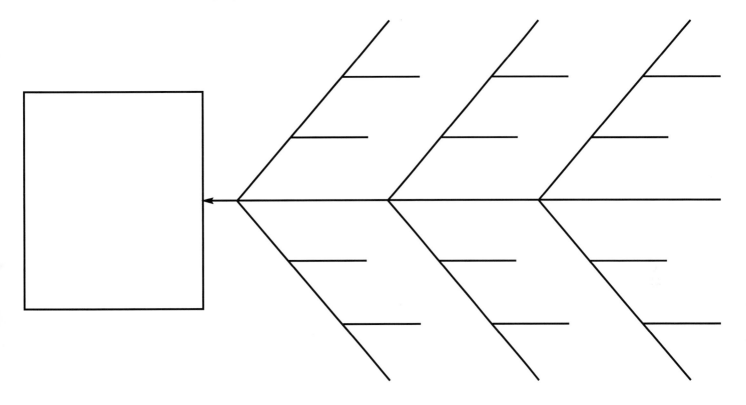

Cycle Diagrams We have looked at two types of organizers in this section, but there are lots of other ways to keep track of causes and effects. Here is another organizer you could use to show cause and effect. Experiment with different ways to use graphic organizers and find the ones that work best for you.

Use this organizer to show how a series of events produces a cyclical set of results. Write the events in order on the lines. Add or delete lines and boxes as needed.

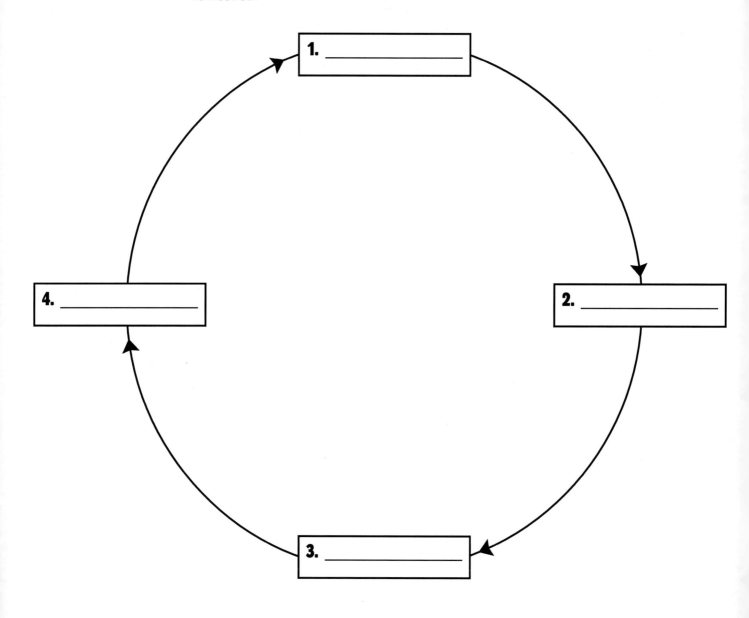

Showing Story Sequence and Character Development

Most stories involve a character with a problem, or conflict. Our job as readers is to recognize the problem and how the characters solve it. All stories revolve around the discovery of the problem or conflict, and the conflict's resolution.

The plot is the "what happens" of a story, a novel, or a play. The plot usually consists of three main parts: the rising action, the climax, and the falling action or resolution.

The rising action is the earliest part of the story in which the conflict is established. This is where we meet the main character or characters, and find out what the problem is. This part of the story is called the rising action because it feels as if everything is building up to one moment. This moment is the climax.

The climax is the most intense emotional moment of the story. It is the turning point toward the resolution or falling action.

The falling action is the third part of the story. This is where the tension of climax begins to subside. This is also where the conflict is resolved.

A graphic organizer is a great way to map out the plot of a story. You can use a plot outline or a story map to show the three main elements of a story. In this lesson, you'll learn how to create and work with a story map.

All stories have characters. Without them, the story would be quite dull! Just as a story's plot has predictable action, so a character goes through changes in a story. In every story, a character changes. You can create a map that shows character changes to understand what makes the character do what he or she does and why. In this lesson, you will also learn how to map a character and his or her changes.

Story Maps   A story or plot map is a visual summary of the story. You can use this map to mark the three main parts of a novel, a short story, or any other piece of fiction. Story maps are very helpful in sorting out the important events of the story. Using a story map combines the skills you already have for finding the main idea, details, and cause and effect.

Using Story Maps   You create a story map by answering important questions about the action of the story. The most important question to answer is, "What is the basic problem (or conflict) in the story?" Next, you will identify which events are most important to the story and how these events lead up to the climax. Finally, you will need to ask yourself: How was the problem solved, or how was the conflict resolved?

Here's a sample story map. The number of events will vary according to the story you are reading.

Main problem or conflict: _____

Character(s) involved in the conflict: _____

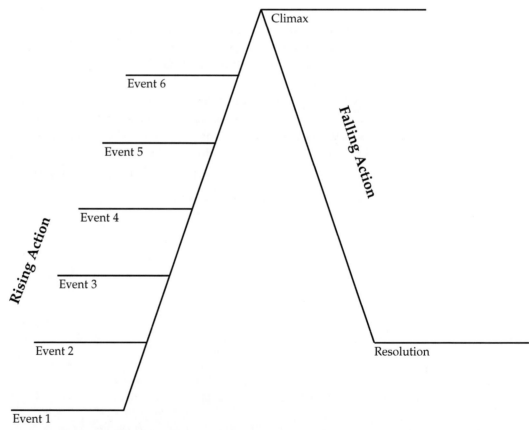

Here is a story collected by folklorists Jakob and Wilhelm Grimm. Read it, then see how the plot is mapped according to the few events that happen in the story.

The Old Grandfather and His Grandson

There was once a very old man, whose eyes had become dim, his ears dull of hearing, his knees trembled. When he sat at the table he could hardly hold the spoon, and spilt the broth upon the table-cloth or let it run out of his mouth. His son and his son's wife were disgusted at this, so the old grandfather at last had to sit in the corner behind the stove, and they gave him his food in an earthenware bowl, and not even enough of it. And he used to look toward the table with his eyes full of tears. Once his shaking hands could not hold the bowl, and it fell to the ground and broke. The young wife scolded him, but he said nothing and only sighed. Then they bought him a wooden bowl for a few half-pence, out of which he had to eat.

They were once sitting thus when the little grandson of four years old began to gather together some bits of wood upon the ground. "What are you doing there?" asked the father. "I am making a little trough," answered the child, "for father and mother to eat out of when I am big."

The man and his wife looked at each other for a while, and presently began to cry. Then they took the old grandfather to the table, and henceforth always let him eat with them, and likewise said nothing if he did spill a little of anything.

Main problem or conflict: Grandfather has become such a messy eater that his son and his son's wife won't let him eat at the table.

Character(s) involved in the conflict: Grandfather, father, mother, grandson

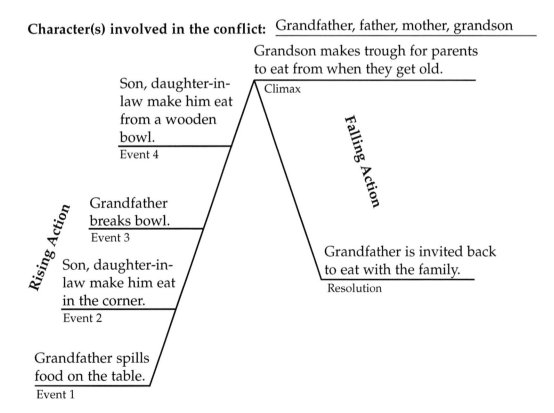

Application   Now it's your turn to create a story map. Read the story below about how Arthur became king of England. Once you have read it, plot the events on the story map on page 47.

How a Boy Became a King

When Uther Pendragon, king of all Britons, died, there was no one to take his place—or so everyone thought. Only a few people knew that Uther did indeed have a son—the rightful king—named Arthur. When he was born, Arthur was whisked away to escape a curse placed on him by a wicked sorceress. Arthur grew up believing he was the son of Sir Ector, a brave knight. Arthur also believed that Sir Ector's son Kay was his brother. While Arthur was growing up with Ector and Kay, he was visited by the wizard Merlin. Merlin taught Arthur how to be gentle and noble, and how to be a great knight.

When Uther died, all the barons and knights wanted to be king. Merlin arranged for a tournament where the noblemen could joust against one another, vying for the title of bravest and best knight. When the noblemen arrived at the town where the tournament was to be held, they saw a huge stone in the town square. An elegant sword was buried to the hilt in the stone. Next to the sword was a message: "Whosoever pulls this sword from the stone is the rightful king of Britain." All the knights wanted that sword to be theirs. They tried to pull the sword from the stone, but all failed.

The only one who knew nothing of the sword was Arthur. He was at the tournament, acting as Kay's squire. When Kay found that he had left his sword at the inn, he asked Arthur to get it for him. Arthur tried to find it, but could not; he did not want to return to Kay empty-handed. As he passed through the town square he saw the sword sticking out of the stone. He climbed up on the rock and pulled the sword gently from its place.

He raced back to Kay and handed him the sword. When Kay asked him where he got it, Arthur confessed that he couldn't find Kay's own sword, and pulled this one out of the stone in the square. Kay, of course, knew that the sword was the magic one that would determine the rightful king. He lied and told his father that it was he who pulled it from the stone. But when Sir Ector saw the sword, he knew that Arthur was the one who took the sword from the stone. Arthur was heralded as the new king; with him came a time of peace and prosperity for England.

Story Map Use the story map below to map the rising action, climax, and falling action of the story on page 46.

Write the events of the rising action on the lines. Add or delete lines as needed. Write the climax on the line at the top of the story map. Write a brief description of the resolution on the line at the base of the story map.

Main problem or conflict: _____

Characters involved in the conflict: _____

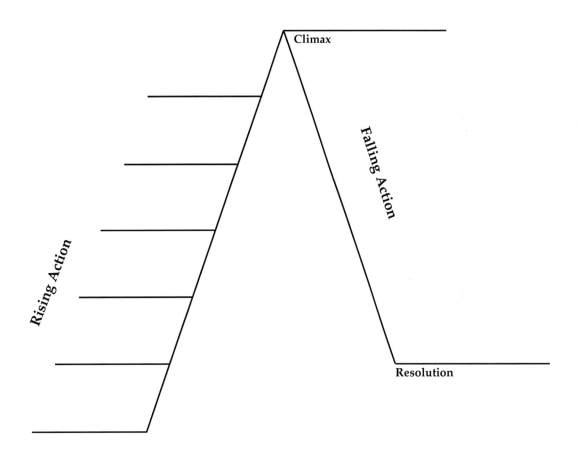

Character Development Maps

Using Character Development Maps

Understanding the way characters change, or develop, in a story, a novel, or a play is part of understanding the story itself.

You can plot the development of a character by using a graphic organizer called a character development map. This is a great way to chart the character's changes and how they relate to the plot.

In *A Christmas Carol*, Ebenezer Scrooge is very stingy and mean. When he is visited by the ghost of his dead business partner, Jacob Marley, he is warned that if he doesn't change his ways, he will be doomed to carry a long, heavy chain after death. His only hope of being free of the chain and of misery is to change his ways and become kind and generous. Marley's ghost wants Scrooge to change so he sends three spirits to show Scrooge his past, his present, and what his future will be if he doesn't change.

To understand a character's development, you need to study how a character changes from the beginning of the story to the end of the story. The best way to do this is to look at the character's actions and feelings. When you plot the character's development, ask yourself two sets of questions. The first set focuses on the character's actions.

1. How does the character act at the beginning of the story?

2. What causes the character to change in the story?

3. How does the character act differently at the end of the story?

The second set of questions has to do with how the character feels. Often you can infer what a character feels from the way he or she acts.

1. How does the character feel at the beginning of the story?

2. How does the character change in the story?

3. How does the character feel at the end of the story?

48

Character Development Maps in Action

Now you can put your answers to these questions into a graphic organizer. All you need to do is jot down a word or a phrase to describe the character's actions and feelings. You may also want to jot down the places where you find evidence for these feelings or actions.

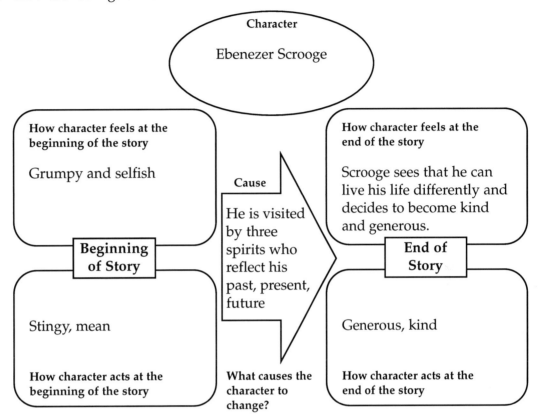

Character

Ebenezer Scrooge

How character feels at the beginning of the story

Grumpy and selfish

Beginning of Story

Stingy, mean

How character acts at the beginning of the story

Cause

He is visited by three spirits who reflect his past, present, future

What causes the character to change?

How character feels at the end of the story

Scrooge sees that he can live his life differently and decides to become kind and generous.

End of Story

Generous, kind

How character acts at the end of the story

Application   Now it's your turn to fill out a character development map. Read the following story. Then fill in the character development map on page 51. Remember to ask yourself the questions you saw on page 48. What is the change that takes place in Jake? What causes him to change?

On Top of the World

Jake Liscars had always been afraid of heights. Ever since he was six, when his father took him up Mt. O'Halloran, he had squirmed every time he found himself higher than the fifth floor. The climb up the mountain had begun as an adventure. But then when Jake slipped on some wet rock and hurtled down the slippery mountainside, he had decided never to climb again. It's not that he got badly hurt. He was just scared, scared for life.

Jake had been able to avoid heights for most of his sixteen years. But now his classmates had planned a year-end campout, and he had no choice but to go. For weeks, his friends talked of nothing else. They were going to climb Mt. Niblock—the highest point in the state. All of them would climb—together as a team.

The day came, and the class arrived at the campout full of anticipation. That first night, everyone was relaxed and sang songs around the campfire. But Jake was thinking just one thing: What if he couldn't make it up the mountain the next day?

It was a long night, but still Jake was startled when his teacher Ms. Osaka stood outside the tent and called out, "Rise and shine, folks, we've got a mountain to climb!"

The climb began effortlessly, and Jake found himself relaxing as they climbed a well-groomed trail. During a trailside lunch, he found himself laughing with his friends. Maybe this mountain would be different from Mt. O'Halloran. Maybe the trees would keep him safe from that panicky feeling.

After lunch, the climb was getting harder, but still Jake felt relieved that there didn't seem to be any rocks ahead. Then, suddenly, the trail curved around and opened out to a sunny, rocky place. Some of the class was already there, and he could hear them say, "Whoa, this is awesome! You can see forever up here! Wow, we're practically in the clouds!"

Jake stepped out into the sunlight. His legs turned rubbery, and he was dizzy and breathless. Just then, Ms. Osaka came up behind him. "Oh boy," she said, "I remember when I was really scared of heights. I used to get such an awful feeling whenever I was high up."

"Really?" Jake asked.

"Oh yes, it wasn't until I was about your age that I finally got over it. I had to go on a trip to the Empire State Building with my class and knew I couldn't get out of it. I didn't feel very brave, but I went anyway."

"What happened?" Jake was really listening.

"I realized that I had a choice. I could either let the fear be in charge, or I could be in charge. So I decided to be in charge. I was scared, but I didn't let that fear stop me. I made it to the top of the building. And you can't imagine how I felt that night. I knew that I was in charge of my fear from then on."

Ms. Osaka's words punched Jake hard. He took a deep breath and said to himself, "OK, fear, it's me and you." He turned and kept climbing until he got to the top of Mt. Niblock. From the top, he could see for miles. He was in charge. He was on top of the world.

Character Development Map

Use this character development map to show how Jake changed over the course of the story.

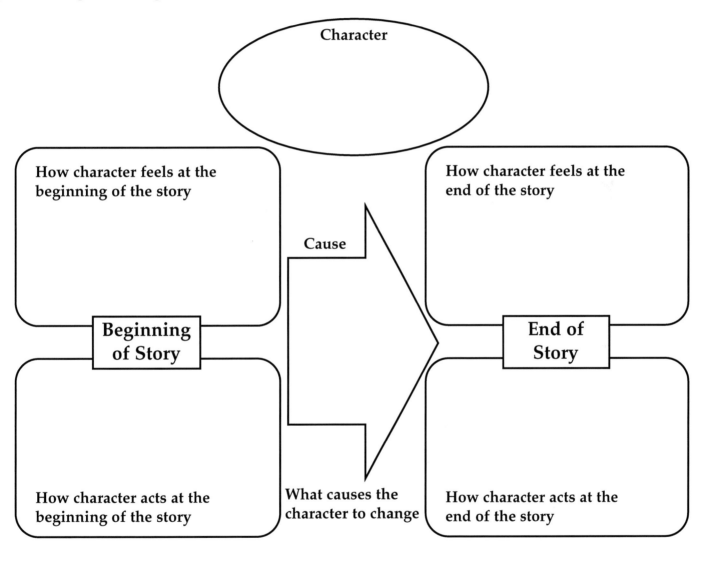

Character

How character feels at the beginning of the story

How character acts at the beginning of the story

Beginning of Story

Cause

What causes the character to change

How character feels at the end of the story

How character acts at the end of the story

End of Story

Content-Area Graphic Organizers: Language Arts

Character Webs We have explored two types of organizers in this section, but there are lots of other ways to show character development. Here is another organizer you could use to show sequence and development. Experiment with different ways to set up graphic organizers to find the ones that work best for you.

Write the character's name in the trapezoid at the top. Write one character trait in each oval, and add a supporting detail in each rectangle. Include page numbers for the details. Add or delete shapes and lines as needed.

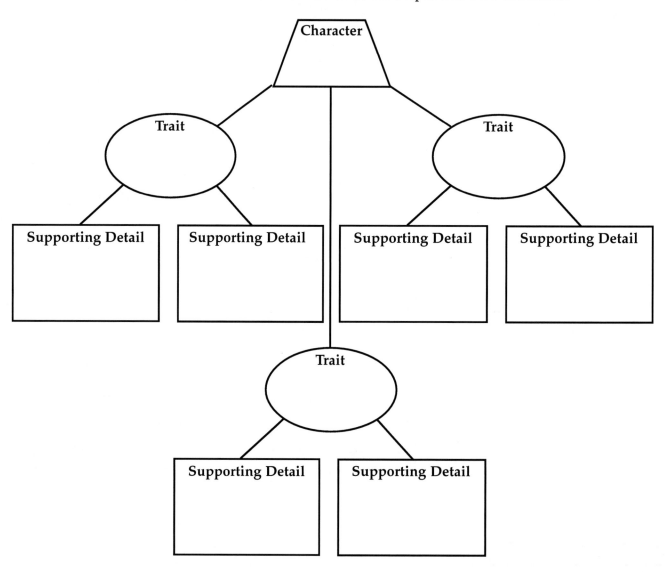

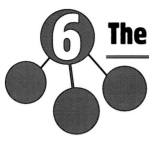

The Writing Process

As you have learned, graphic organizers are very helpful when you are reading. But they can also improve your writing skills. In this lesson, you'll learn how to use webs to improve your brainstorming, planning, and writing. Whether you're writing a poem, an essay, a story, a review, or even a journal entry, graphic organizers can help!

Graphic organizers are a great tool in the writing process. The writing process helps writers organize their thoughts. It also helps writers avoid frustration and use their time efficiently. The steps for the writing process begin with creating a free flow of ideas. The process ends when a piece has been written, revised, proofread, and "published," or completed.

Step one in the writing process is prewriting. This is the brainstorming and planning stage before you begin to write. It is an important part of your writing because it helps you organize your thoughts and plan what you want to express in your writing.

The first thing you do in prewriting is to create a free flow of ideas, or brainstorm. Using a brainstorming web, you can collect all the ideas you have about your writing topic. In this lesson, you'll learn how to use a web to improve your skills.

The next step in prewriting is planning. This is the stage at which you decide what you want to include in your writing and what you can leave out, based on your brainstorming ideas. This is also when you decide what supporting details to include. At this stage, you can use an outline to plan your writing.

Once you've finished the prewriting, it is time to start writing. Graphic organizers can help with that, too. For the writing stage, you can use an expository writing organizer. This is a more detailed outline, that contains some of the sentences you want to include in your writing. This is a place where you can begin to do some preliminary editing of unnecessary information or story elements.

Brainstorming Webs

There are two brainstorming techniques you can use to improve your writing. You can brainstorm to find a topic to write about, or to generate ideas for a topic you have already chosen. Brainstorming is rarely neat and tidy. This is the time to just let the ideas flow. There are no strict rules for brainstorming. Anything goes. You'll be able to edit your ideas later.

One good way to brainstorm is to set aside a specific amount of time—such as five minutes. As you brainstorm, try not to dismiss ideas as silly or wrong. Just keep writing until the time is up. Don't worry about being neat. You can brainstorm all over a sheet of paper. Just be sure you can read it when you go back to it! Once you've completed your brainstorming session, review what you wrote. Then circle, highlight, or jot down the words and phrases that you want to develop in your writing.

Using Brainstorming Webs

A brainstorming web is a great tool to use as you organize your thoughts. You begin by drawing a circle in the center of your paper. In that circle, write the main topic or idea you are brainstorming. If you are preparing to write something creative, then you can put the topic in the middle. For example, let's say your teacher asks you to write a poem about spring. The word "spring" would go in the middle of your web. Then you would surround the word "spring" with lines drawn away from the circle. At the end of the lines, draw circles for images, words, ideas, or thoughts you have about spring.

If you are asked to write an informational essay about a topic, you write that topic in the middle of your web. For example, let's say your teacher asks you to write a paper on the life of Harriet Tubman. You would begin your brainstorming by writing anything you know about Harriet Tubman. Then, as you learn more, you can add to the circles. Later you can discard ideas that are not important and decide what ideas will be your focus.

Brainstorming Webs in Action

Here is an example of a brainstorming web for a poem about spring. Notice how many ideas are generated about spring. Even though the writer won't use all of these ideas, once the brainstorming session is over, there will be lots of ideas from which to choose.

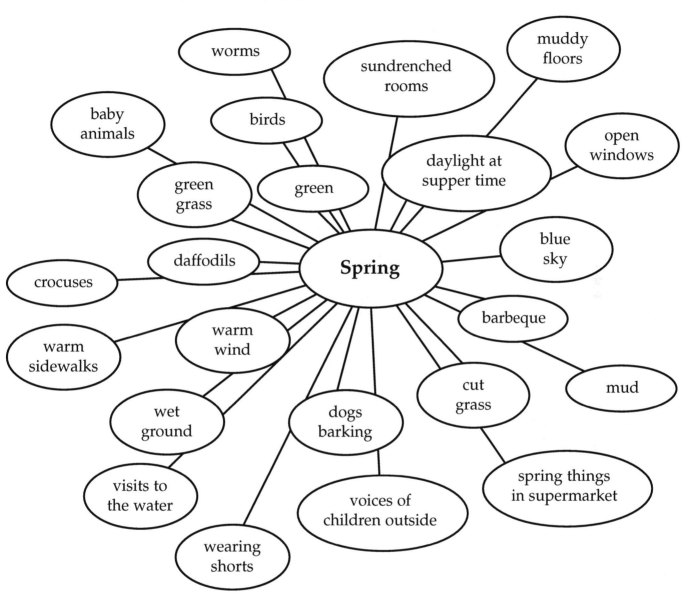

Application Imagine that your teacher has asked you to write a paper about one of the topics below. Choose one of them. Then use the brainstorming web on page 57 to generate ideas about your topic. You should already know something about most of the topics, but you should also do some additional research.

Topic 1: Compare and contrast the main characters of two short stories or novels you have read in the last several months. Be sure to include a variety of characteristics, such as a description of each character's physical appearance, behavior, personality traits, and feelings.

Topic 2: Write a short biography of one of your favorite authors. Begin by creating a web of what you already know about the author and then do some research to find out more. Add your researched material to your web. Include some information on why this author became a writer.

Topic 3: Some writers are both poets and novelists. What are some of the differences in the process of writing poems versus writing prose? What are some similarities?

Topic 4: Choose two books to compare and contrast the problems, or conflicts, in each story. How are they similar? How are they different? How does the main character in each story deal with the problem?

Topic 5: What is your favorite book? Why?

Topic 6: Many books are made into movies; for example, J.K. Rowling's *Harry Potter and the Sorcerer's Stone*, J.R.R. Tolkien's *The Lord of the Rings*, Harper Lee's *To Kill a Mockingbird*, or Alice Walker's *The Color Purple*. Choose a movie based on a book and compare and contrast each version of the story. Did the movie follow the book closely? Which do you prefer?

Topic 7: Choose a piece of art with which you are familiar or find one in a book. Write a story based on what you think is happening in the work of art. Do some research to include why the artist chose to create this piece of art.

Topic 8: Write a poem about someone who is very special to you. Focus on your feelings, and be sure to include the five senses in your poem.

Topic 9: Write an essay that discusses your opinion on war. Do you agree or disagree with it as a way to settle differences? Be sure to support your statements with specific examples.

Topic 10: Write an autobiography of your life in the form of a song, a poem, an essay, or a story. Begin with images and words that describe your early life, and include information up to the present.

Brainstorming Web Use this web to brainstorm ideas about the writing topic you chose. Add circles as needed.

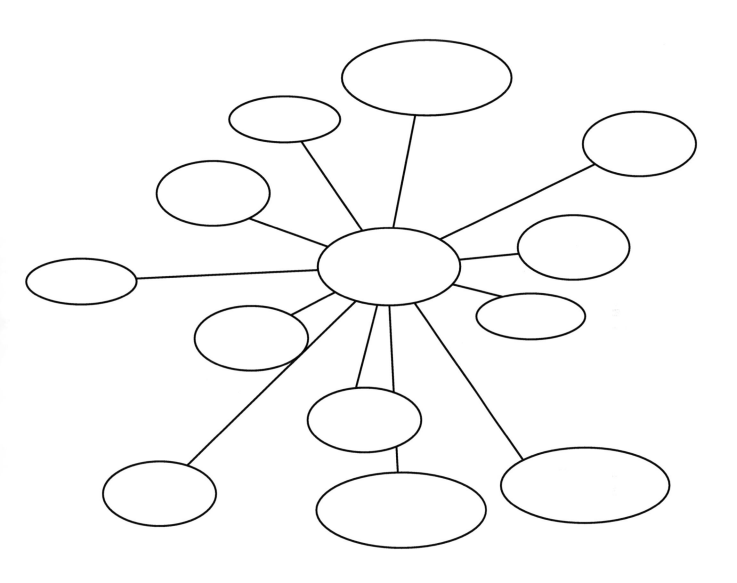

Outlines Now that you've brainstormed about your writing topic, it's time to create a plan for writing, called an outline. An outline is an organized overview of the main ideas for your writing topic. The purpose of an outline is to help you organize and simplify your ideas. Use it to plan the beginning, middle, and conclusion of your work, as well as the transitions between them.

An outline should be divided into three or four main headings. These represent the main points you want to make. Under each heading there are supporting details. Sometimes even the supporting details have details.

Before you begin an outline, you need to be sure that you know the answers to these three questions:

1. What is my purpose for writing? (Is it to entertain, inform, persuade, or describe?)

2. Who is my audience? (Am I writing for myself? for publication? for a class assignment? for a test?)

3. What is the main idea? (Is it informational? If so, what is the point I want to make? Is it narrative or descriptive? If so, then what do I want my reader to know about my idea or topic?)

Once you have answered these questions, you can look at your brainstorming notes and decide what to keep and what to discard. You can begin the outlining process by circling, highlighting, or jotting down the ideas from your brainstorming session. Which are the main ideas you want to write about?

Outlines can be either informal or formal. We'll look at informal outlines a little later.

Using Formal Outlines

A formal outline is used mostly in informational or expository writing. It follows a very specific pattern. It includes Roman numerals to list the main ideas, and letters to list the subtopics to support the main ideas. Regular numbers list the details to support the subtopics. A formal outline pattern looks like this:

Title

I. Introduction

    A. Opening statement—attention grabber

    B. Main idea or thesis

II. First topic

    A. Subtopic

        1. Evidence or example

        2. Evidence or example

    B. Subtopic

        1. Evidence or example

        2. Evidence or example

III. Second topic

    A. Subtopic

        1. Evidence or example

        2. Evidence or example

    B. Subtopic

        1. Evidence or example

        2. Evidence or example

IV. Conclusion

    A. Restatement of main idea

    B. Final statement

Generally, an outline follows this pattern. However, the number of topics, subtopics, and examples may vary. There are two important features of an outline: You don't necessarily need complete sentences, only short, descriptive phrases, except in the introduction and conclusion. And if you have one subtopic, or example, you must have at least two. In other words, where there's an A, there's a B. Where there's a 1, there's a 2.

Let's say that your teacher has asked you to write a biography of Charlotte Brontë. You have brainstormed your topic based on your research, and you are ready to make an outline. Here's how you might answer the three questions:

1. What is my purpose for writing? *I want to describe the life of Charlotte Brontë.*

2. Who is my audience? *I am writing for my teacher and for the rest of my class. I am also writing to understand the way an author's life is reflected in his or her work.*

3. What is the main idea? What point do I want to make? *I want to show that Charlotte Brontë had a difficult childhood and a life filled with grief, but she still managed to write one of the best-known books of all time.*

Here is an example of how you might prepare an outline for this topic.

Charlotte Brontë and Her Best-Known Work

I. Introduction

    A. Opening statement: Charlotte Brontë lived a grief-filled life.

    B. Main idea: Even though her life was difficult, Charlotte Brontë was driven to write and penned one of the greatest British novels, *Jane Eyre.*

II. Early life

    A. Mother died when she was young

    B. Was sent away to school where teachers were cruel

    C. Two older sisters died of tuberculosis.

    D. Her strict aunt came to live with her.

III. Early writing

    A. Created an imaginary world with her brother and sister

    B. Wrote poetry and stories about "Gandal"

    C. Published stories and poems using pen name

IV. Working life

    A. Worked as governess

    B. Worked as teacher

    C. Fell in love with married headmaster

V. *Jane Eyre*

    A. Includes story about governess and teacher

    B. Reflects love between Jane and Rochester—not realized, just like her own love with the headmaster

    C. Is very successful

VI. Conclusion

    A. Ms. Brontë's grief and sadness is woven into her work.

    B. Even though odds were against her, Ms. Brontë managed to write a hugely successful book still widely read today.

Application Now it's your turn to prepare an outline. On page 56, you chose a topic to write about and created a brainstorming web. Now transfer ideas about your topic to the outline below.

Topic   I. _____

   Subtopic   A. _____

      Supporting   1. _____
      details   2. _____
                   3. _____
                   4. _____

   Subtopic   B. _____

      Supporting   1. _____
      details   2. _____
                   3. _____
                   4. _____

   Subtopic   C. _____

      Supporting   1. _____
      details   2. _____
                   3. _____
                   4. _____

   Subtopic   D. _____

      Supporting   1. _____
      details   2. _____
                   3. _____
                   4. _____

Informal Outlines

Like a formal outline, an informal outline gives an overview of the way the paper will be developed. Unlike a formal outline, it does not use a system of Roman numerals, capital letters, and Arabic numerals. An informal outline may use short phrases, or it may use complete sentences . It includes an indication of how each supporting statement will be developed, such as by using examples, descriptions, comparisons, and so forth. An informal outline often begins with a thesis statement—a statement of what the essay is designed to show. Now choose another topic from page 56, create a brainstorming web, and then use this informal outline to organize your ideas..

Thesis statement:

Support statement 1:

Developed by:

Support statement 2:

Developed by:

Support statement 3:

Developed by:

Support statement 4:

Developed by:

Conclusion:

Developed by:

Expository Writing Organizers

Formal and informal outlines are two ways to approach organizing a writing assignment. Another graphic organizer that can help you is an expository writing organizer.

An expository writing organizer is a great way to lay out most of your work before you start writing. Like an outline, an expository writing organizer can be formal or informal. The formal organizer has headings for paragraphs, much like an outline. However, the expository writing organizer includes full sentences that you can incorporate directly into your writing.

Imagine that your teacher has asked you to write a paper on how a poet laureate is chosen for the United States. Here is a brainstorm of the facts. Look on page 65 to see how the facts have been translated into an expository writing chart.

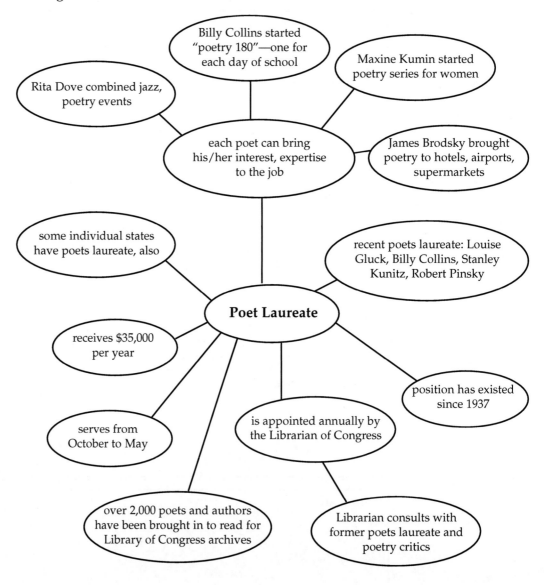

Expository Writing Charts

An expository writing chart looks like the model below. The chart has been filled in using the information from the brainstorming web on page 64.

Opening sentences:
Each year, the Librarian of Congress appoints a poet to be Poet Laureate of the United States.

These poets are chosen by former laureates and by poetry critics.

They serve one term, from October to May. They are paid $35,000 a year. They often bring other poets into the library for a reading. More than 2,000 poets have been brought through the library since the beginning of the poet laureate program.

Transition word or phrase:
Each poet is unique.

Paragraph 1: Topic sentence: The poets laureate can bring their own special interests to the job.

Supporting details:
1. Billy Collins created a "poetry 180" project to introduce students to a new poem every day of the school year.
2. James Brodsky brought poetry to hotels, airports, and supermarkets.
3. Maxine Kumin started a poetry series for women.

Transition word or phrase:
Some states also have poets laureate.

Paragraph 2: Topic sentence: Some states have poets laureate as well. They are appointed for a longer time than national laureates.

Supporting details:
1. example of ways that state poets have served their states
2. how to find out if there is a state laureate in your state

Conclusion:
The job of poet laureate helps expose people throughout the country to great poets and their work.

Expository Writing Map, Model A

Here's another version of an expository writing organizer. See if you can take the information from the organizer on page 65 and plug it into the organizer below. Which organizer style do you prefer? It's important to remember that you should use the style of organizer that works best for you.

Write the topic sentence for a paragraph in the center circle. Write details in the smaller circles. Use a separate organizer for each paragraph. Write your conclusion in the last box.

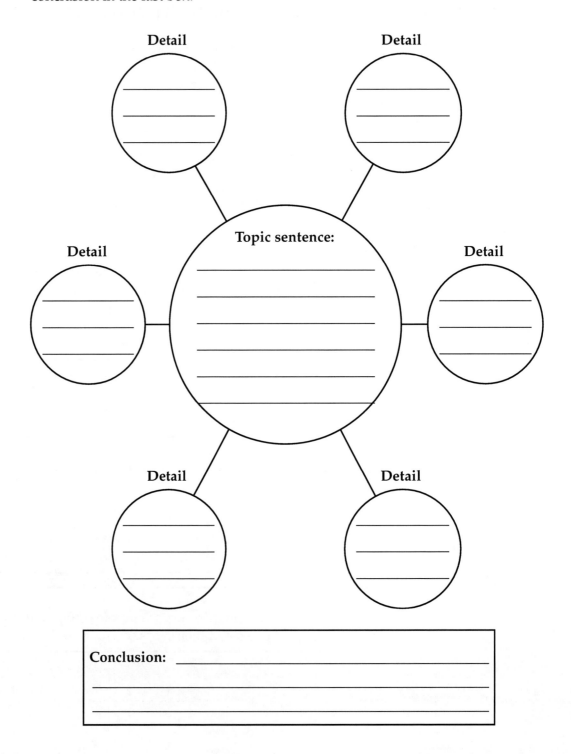

Expository Writing Map, Model B

We have looked at several types of writing organizers in this section, but there are lots of other ways to organize writing. Here is another organizer you can use for your writing. Experiment with different ways to set up graphic organizers.

Write the main idea in the center circle. Write a topic sentence in each outer circle. Write supporting details on the lines around each circle.

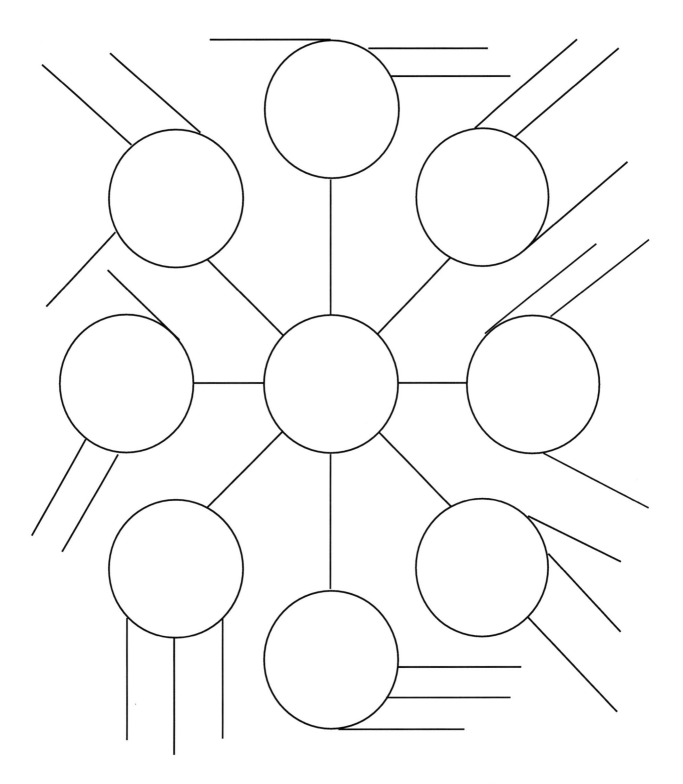

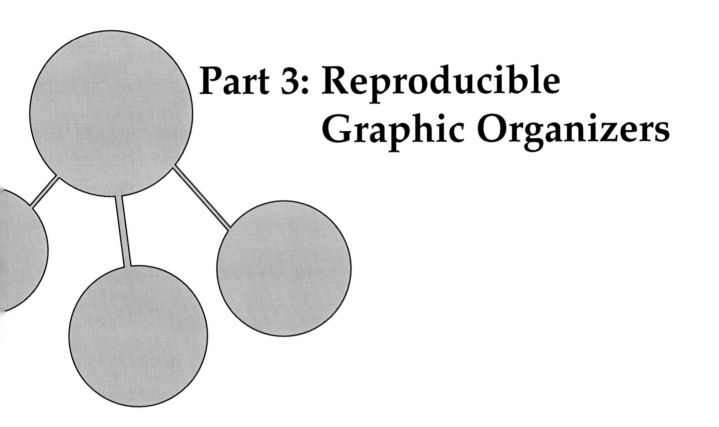

Part 3: Reproducible
Graphic Organizers

Web

Write your topic in the center circle. Then write details in the smaller circles. Add and delete lines and circles as needed.

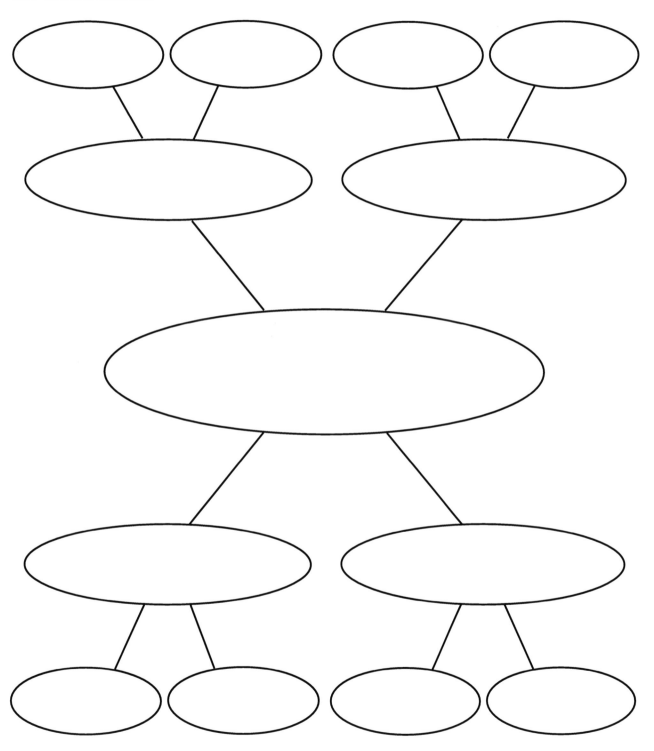

Write the categories for your information at the top of the columns. Then record the information in the columns. Add or delete columns as needed. You may also want to add horizontal lines.

Main Idea and Details Chart

Write one main idea in each box across the top. Write supporting details in the smaller boxes. Add or delete boxes as needed.

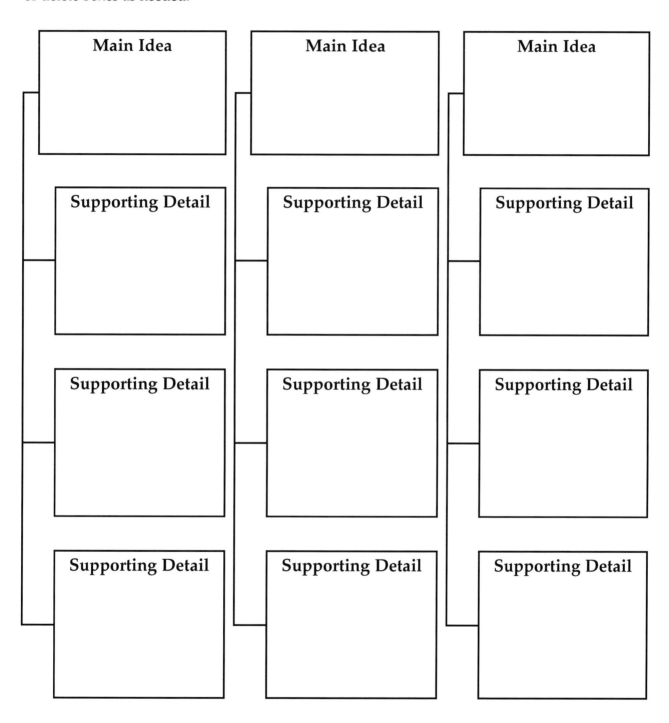

Spider Map

Write the topic or theme of the reading in the oval. Write one main idea on each diagonal line. Write one supporting detail on each horizontal line. Add or delete lines as needed.

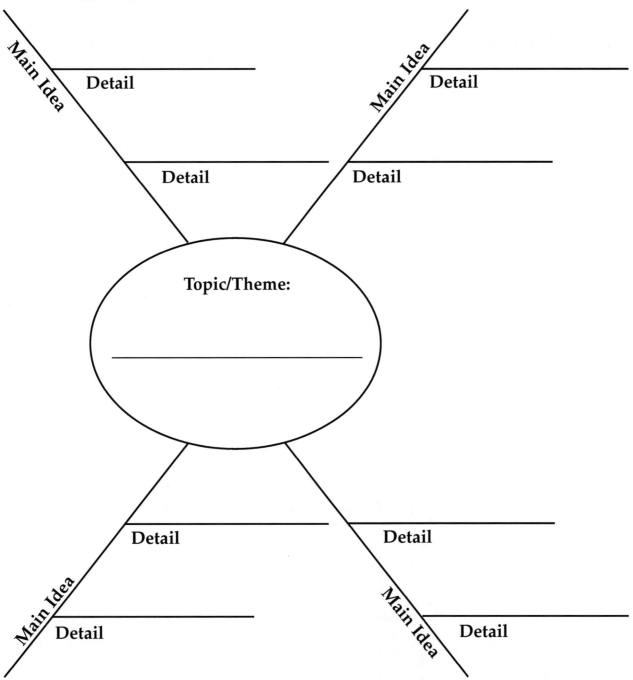

Main Idea

Detail

Detail

Main Idea

Detail

Detail

Topic/Theme:

_____

Detail

Detail

Main Idea

Detail

Main Idea

Detail

Venn Diagram

Label each circle. Write things that are unique to each topic in the open area of each circle. Write things both topics have in common in the intersecting area.

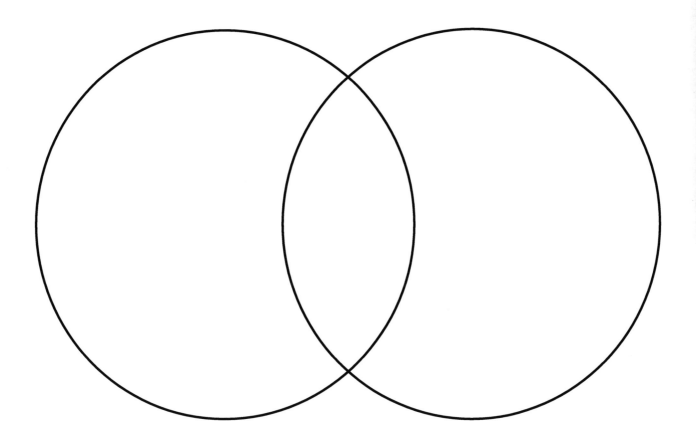

75

Write the characteristics to be compared across the top. Write the items to be compared at the beginning of each row. Add or delete rows and columns as needed. Then put checkmarks in the boxes where rows and columns meet to show that an item has a certain characteristic.

Compare and Contrast Diagram

Write the things you are comparing on the lines at the top. In the first box, say how they are alike. Write the characteristics you are contrasting under "With Regard To." Then show how the items are different according to these characteristics.

Item 1 _____   Item 2 _____

How Alike?

How Different?

With Regard To

Cause and Effect Map 1

Use this organizer to show one cause with several effects. Write the cause in the box at the top. Write the effects in the boxes below. Add or delete boxes as needed.

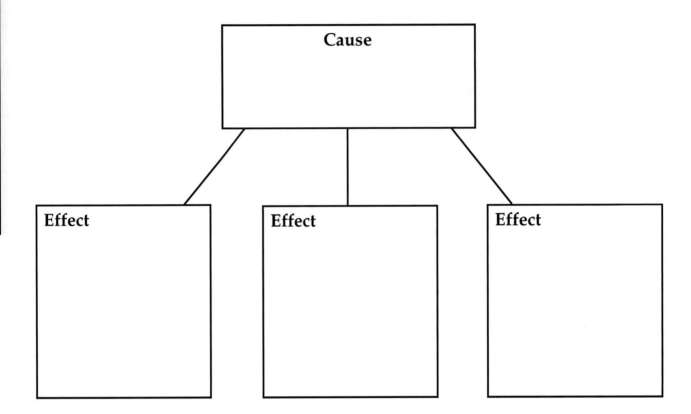

Cause and Effect-Map 2

Use this organizer to show multiple causes and effects. Write each cause in one oval. Write all its effects in the corresponding box. Add or delete ovals and boxes as needed.

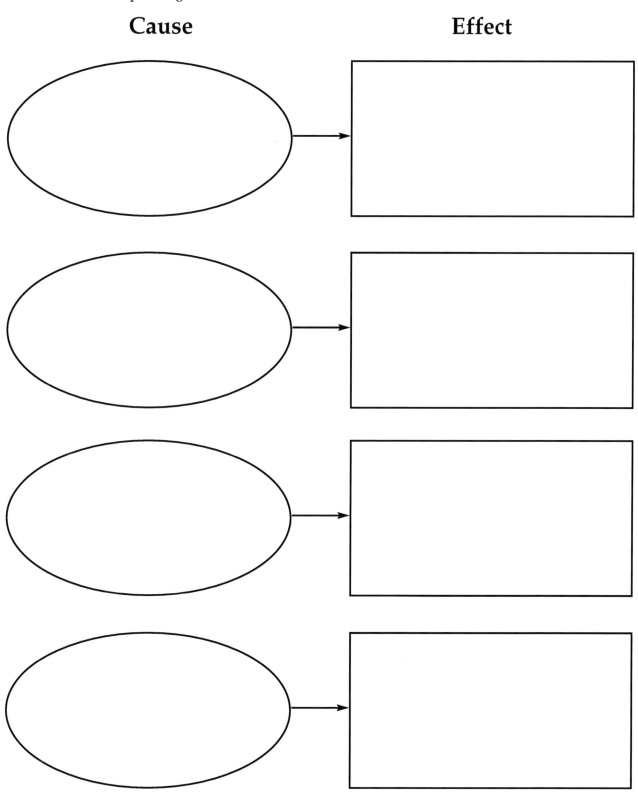

Cause   Effect

Fishbone Map

Write the effect in the box at the left. Write the causes on the diagonal lines. Write details on the short horizontal lines. Add or delete lines as needed.

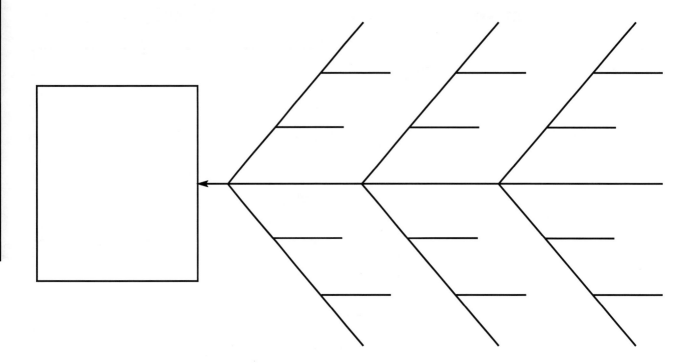

80

Cycle Diagram

Use this organizer to show how a series of events produces a cyclical set of results. Write the events in order on the lines. Add or delete lines and boxes as needed.

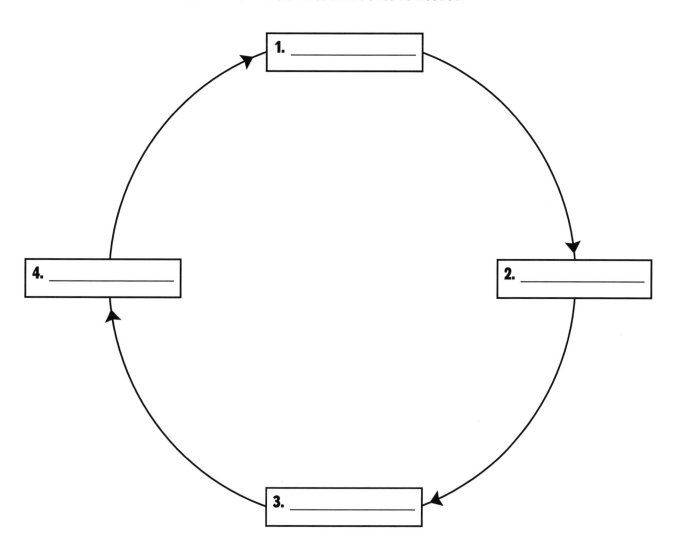

Story Map

First, state the main problem or conflict of the story. Then name the characters involved in the conflict. Next, write the events of the rising action on the lines. Add or delete lines as needed. Write the climax on the line at the top of the story map. Write a brief description of the resolution on the line at the base of the story map.

Main problem or conflict: _____

Character(s) involved in the conflict: _____

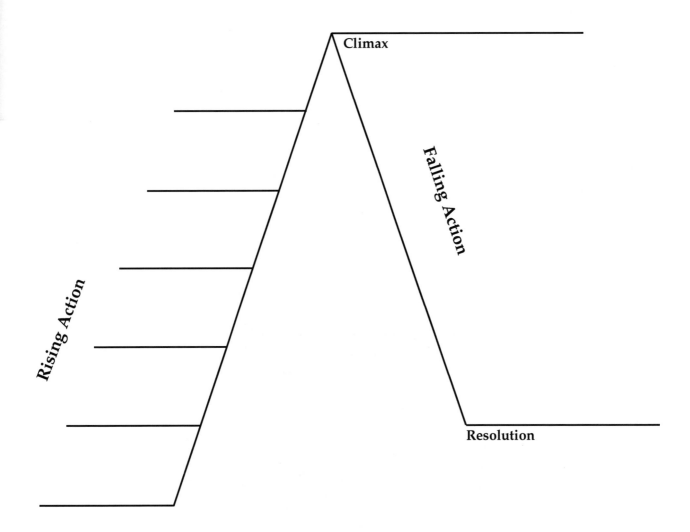

Character Development Map

Write the character's name in the circle. Fill in the character traits and the cause of the change.

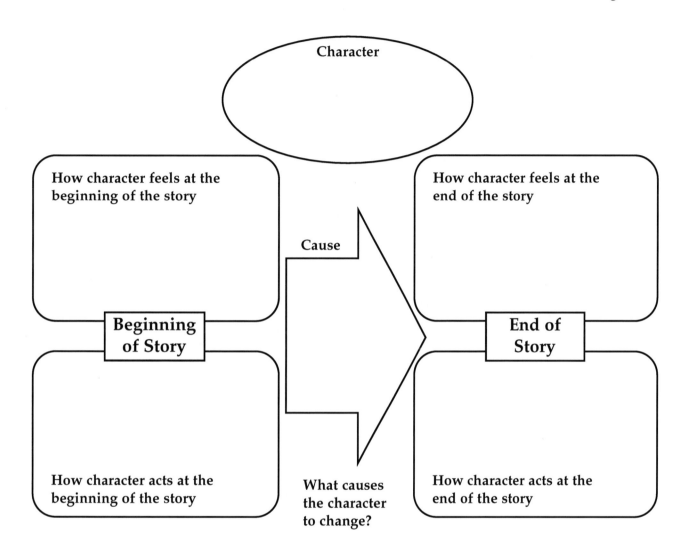

Character

How character feels at the beginning of the story

Cause

Beginning of Story

How character acts at the beginning of the story

What causes the character to change?

How character feels at the end of the story

End of Story

How character acts at the end of the story

Character Web

Write the character's name in the trapezoid at the top. Write one character trait in each oval, and add a supporting detail in each rectangle. Include page numbers for the details. Add or delete shapes and lines as needed.

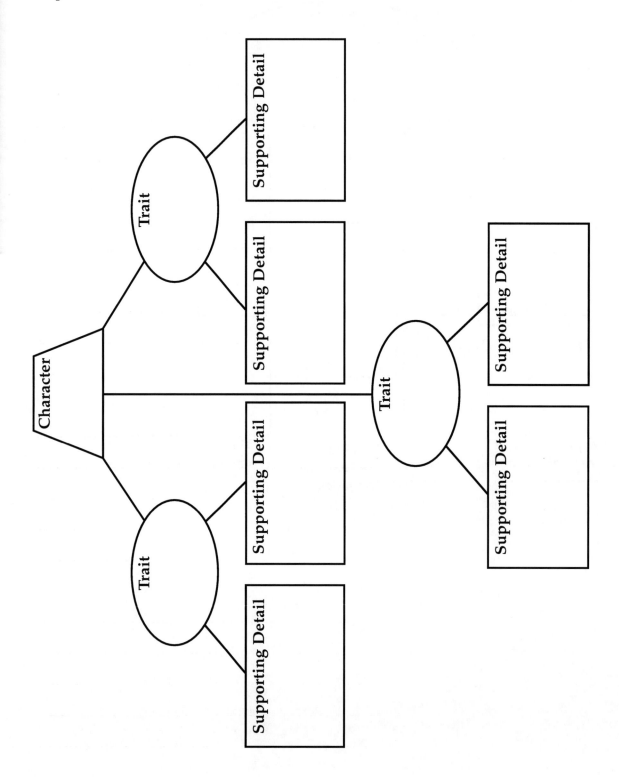

Formal Outline

Write the topic on the line at the top. Then fill in the rest of the outline with subtopics and supporting details.

Topic   I. _____

Subtopic   A. _____

    Supporting   1. _____
    details   2. _____
                        3. _____
                        4. _____

Subtopic   B. _____

    Supporting   1. _____
    details   2. _____
                        3. _____
                        4. _____

Subtopic   C. _____

    Supporting   1. _____
    details   2. _____
                        3. _____
                        4. _____

Subtopic   D. _____

    Supporting   1. _____
    details   2. _____
                        3. _____
                        4. _____

Informal Outline

Use information about your topic to fill in the organizer. Add sections for support statements as needed.

Thesis statement:

Support statement 1:

Developed by:

Support statement 2:

Developed by:

Support statement 3:

Developed by:

Support statement 4:

Developed by:

Conclusion:

Developed by:

Expository Writing Chart

Use information about your topic to fill in the organizer. Add sections for paragraphs, details, and transition words as needed.

Opening sentences:

Transition word or phrase:

Paragraph 1: Topic sentence:

Supporting details:

Transition word or phrase:

Paragraph 2: Topic sentence:

Supporting details:

Conclusion:

Expository Writing Map, Model A

Write the topic sentence for a paragraph in the center circle. Write details in the smaller circles. Use a separate organizer for each paragraph. Write your conclusion in the last box.

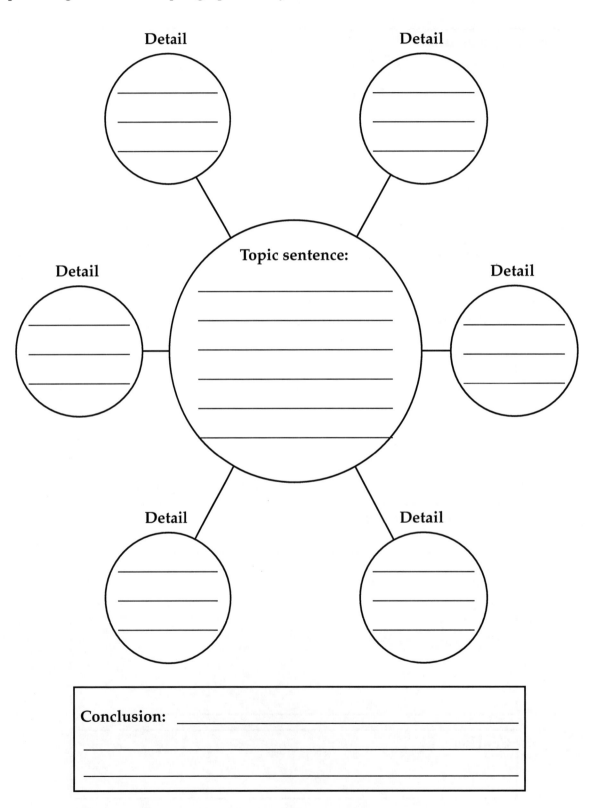

Expository Writing Map, Model B

Write the main idea in the center circle. Write a topic sentence in each outer circle. Write supporting details on the lines around each circle.

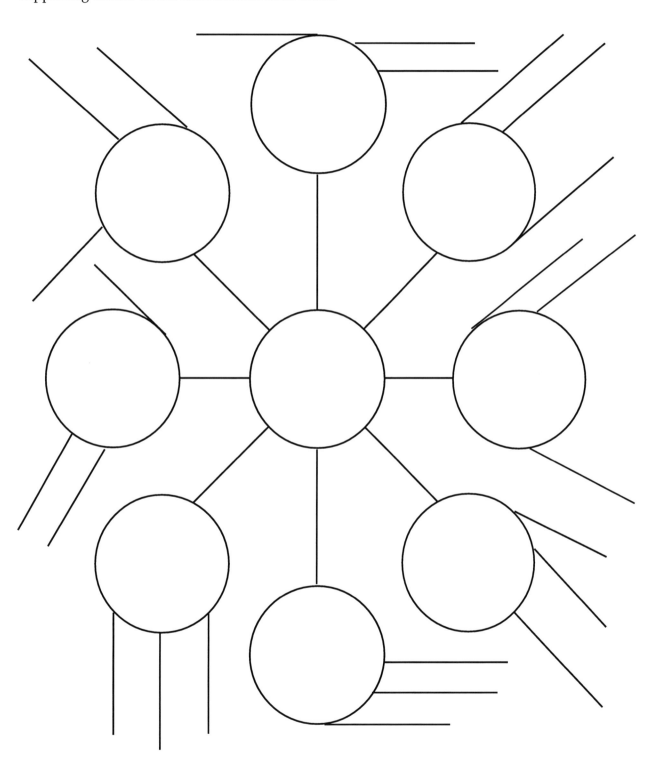

Answer Key

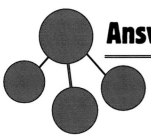

Answer Key: Lesson 2

Web, page 12

The following is an example of how students might fill in the web graphic organizer. Students' answers may vary. Encourage students to choose the most relevant information and put it in the circles around the web. Help them to determine which pieces of information are the most important. One way to help them would be to point out the topic sentences in each paragraph and remind students that the topic sentence often reflects the main idea.

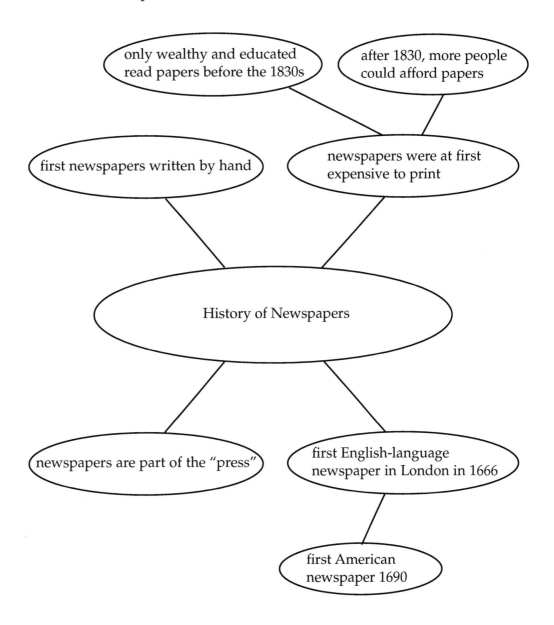

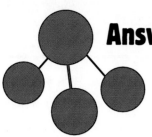

Answer Key: Lesson 2

Chart, page 17

	Hurry Harry	Deerslayer	Evidence
Physical description	over six feet four; very strong, handsome, rugged	six feet; slender and light; agile, young	lines 67–12 lines 14–17
How he dresses	deer-skins; sloppy	neat and tidy	line 24 lines 25–27
Other characteristics	reckless and offhand; always moving	sincere with air of integrity	lines 5–6 lines 18–20
What his personality might be like based on his description	easygoing, secure, quick-witted, smart, noble	sincere	lines 1–3 line 19

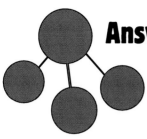

Answer Key: Lesson 2

Main Idea and Details Chart, page 21

Main Idea	**Main Idea**	**Main Idea**
Beryl Markham became a famous horse trainer.	Markham became a famous pilot.	Markham became a famous writer.

Supporting Detail	**Supporting Detail**	**Supporting Detail**
She grew up with horses.	She met pilot Dennis Finch Hatton and learned to fly.	She wrote *West with the Night*, which topped best-seller charts.

Supporting Detail	**Supporting Detail**	**Supporting Detail**
She won a prize and became well known in Kenyan society.	In 1936, she became the first woman to fly across Atlantic; she crash-landed in Nova Scotia.	Praised by Ernest Hemingway

Supporting Detail	**Supporting Detail**	**Supporting Detail**
She returned to horse training when she stopped flying.	She stopped flying when a friend was killed in a plane crash.	Her third husband may have cowritten *West with the Night*.

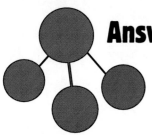

Answer Key: Lesson 3

Venn Diagram, page 27

Answers will vary. Sample answer:

Colleges

Smaller than universities

Most classes taught by college teachers

No graduate students

Only offer bachelor's degree

May be contained within a university

Both

Place you attend after finishing high school/GED

Offer bachelor's degrees—bachelor of arts, bachelor of science

Harder to get into highly ranked schools

Can be private or public

Universities

Larger than colleges

Some classes taught by graduate students

Offer higher degrees, including Ph.D.'s

Faculty often split between teaching, research

May include colleges

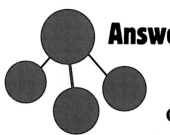

Answer Key: Lesson 3

Comparison Matrix, page 31

	Jim	Will
Attribute 1: Looks	Dark	Fair
Attribute 2: How they act	Impulsive	Deliberate
Attribute 3: How they behave toward others	Not as sensitive as Will	Empathetic

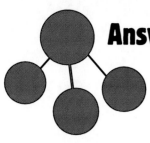

Answer Key: Lesson 4

Cause and Effect Maps, page 37

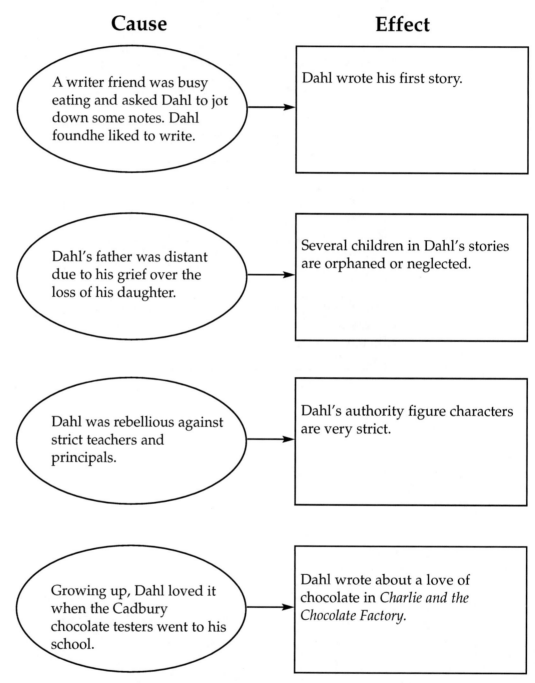

Cause	Effect
A writer friend was busy eating and asked Dahl to jot down some notes. Dahl foundhe liked to write.	Dahl wrote his first story.
Dahl's father was distant due to his grief over the loss of his daughter.	Several children in Dahl's stories are orphaned or neglected.
Dahl was rebellious against strict teachers and principals.	Dahl's authority figure characters are very strict.
Growing up, Dahl loved it when the Cadbury chocolate testers went to his school.	Dahl wrote about a love of chocolate in *Charlie and the Chocolate Factory*.

Answer Key: Lesson 4

Fishbone Map, page 41

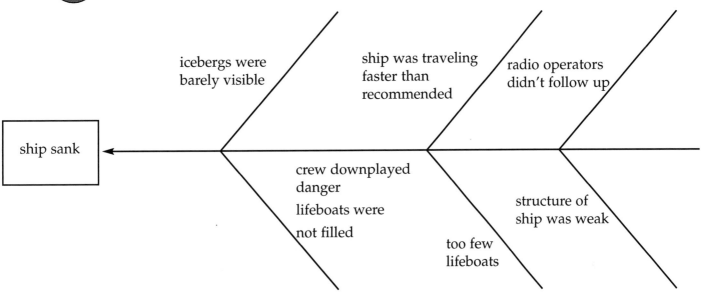

ship sank

icebergs were barely visible

ship was traveling faster than recommended

radio operators didn't follow up

crew downplayed danger

lifeboats were not filled

too few lifeboats

structure of ship was weak

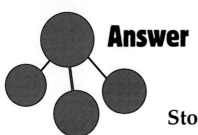

Answer Key: Lesson 5

Story Map, page 47

Main problem or conflict: There is no rightful heir to the throne of Britain.

Characters involved in the conflict: All the knights and nobles of Britain

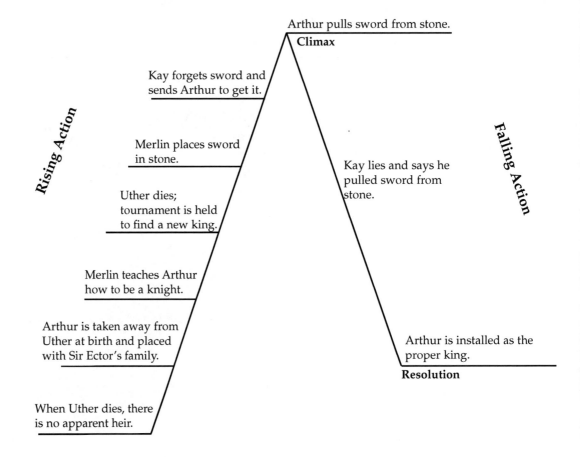

Arthur pulls sword from stone.
Climax

Rising Action

Kay forgets sword and sends Arthur to get it.

Merlin places sword in stone.

Uther dies; tournament is held to find a new king.

Merlin teaches Arthur how to be a knight.

Arthur is taken away from Uther at birth and placed with Sir Ector's family.

When Uther dies, there is no apparent heir.

Falling Action

Kay lies and says he pulled sword from stone.

Arthur is installed as the proper king.
Resolution

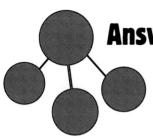

Answer Key: Lesson 5

Character Development Map, page 51

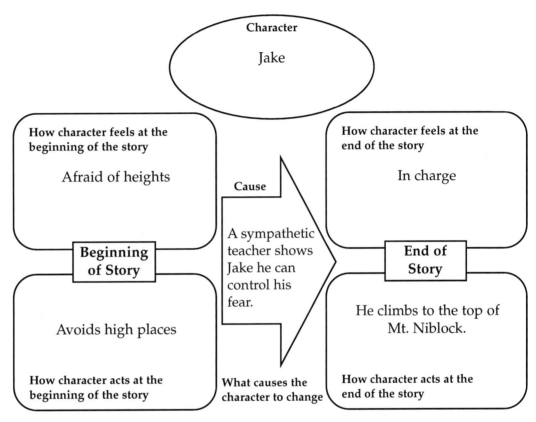

Character

Jake

How character feels at the beginning of the story

Afraid of heights

Beginning of Story

Avoids high places

How character acts at the beginning of the story

Cause

A sympathetic teacher shows Jake he can control his fear.

What causes the character to change

How character feels at the end of the story

In charge

End of Story

He climbs to the top of Mt. Niblock.

How character acts at the end of the story

Share Your Bright Ideas

We want to hear from you!

Your name_____Date_____

School name_____

School address_____

City _____State_____Zip_____Phone number (_____)_____

Grade level(s) taught_____Subject area(s) taught_____

Where did you purchase this publication?_____

In what month do you purchase a majority of your supplements?_____

What moneys were used to purchase this product?

____School supplemental budget ____Federal/state funding ____Personal

Please "grade" this Walch publication in the following areas:

Quality of service you received when purchasing ....A   B   C   D

Ease of use...A   B   C   D

Quality of content..A   B   C   D

Page layout ....A   B   C   D

Organization of material ....A   B   C   D

Suitability for grade level...A   B   C   D

Instructional value...A   B   C   D

COMMENTS:_____

_____

What specific supplemental materials would help you meet your current—or future—instructional needs?

_____

Have you used other Walch publications? If so, which ones?_____

May we use your comments in upcoming communications?   ____Yes   ____No

Please **FAX** this completed form to **888-991-5755**, or mail it to

Customer Service, Walch Publishing, P. O. Box 658, Portland, ME 04104-0658

We will send you a **FREE GIFT** in appreciation of your feedback. **THANK YOU!**